Blueberry Hill

Slow Cooker & Family Recipes

This edition published in 2012
LOVE FOOD is an imprint of Parragon Books Ltd

Parragon Publishing
Queen Street House
4 Queen Street
Bath BA1 1HE, UK

www.parragon.com

ISBN: 978-1-4454-4055-2

Printed in China

Notes for the Reader
This book uses standard kitchen measuring spoons and cups. All spoon and cup measurements are level
unless otherwise indicated. Unless otherwise stated, milk is assumed to be whole, eggs are large,
individual vegetables are medium, and pepper is freshly ground black pepper. Unless otherwise stated, all
root vegetables should be washed and peeled before using.

The times given are only an approximate guide. Preparation times differ according to the techniques used
by different people and the cooking times may also vary from those given. Optional ingredients,
variations, or serving suggestions have not been included in the calculations.

Recipes using raw or very lightly cooked eggs should be avoided by infants, the elderly, pregnant women,
and anyone with a chronic illness. Pregnant and breast-feeding women are advised to avoid eating peanuts
and peanut products. People with nut allergies should be aware that some of the prepared ingredients used
in the recipes in this book may contain nuts. Always check the packaging before use.

Contents

Welcome to Blueberry Hill

Here at Blueberry Hill we understand that busy families need easy and simple solutions. No one has the time to spend hours over a hot stove, when the kids need to be picked up from school, there's a deadline to reach at work and you need to conjure up something from the leftovers in the fridge. The good news is that with our recipes you can still feed your family good, honest, wholesome and nutritious meals but you won't feel like you are tied to your kitchen!

Our books are designed to introduce (or re-introduce) you to healthy, economical, and delicious food. Many of the recipes are lovingly remembered classics, while others feature familiar ingredients prepared from a fresh perspective.

Blueberry Hill Books are produced by a consortium of top-notch cooks and food professionals who have created a collection of hundreds of delectable family-style recipes, from appetizers to desserts. Each and every dish has been carefully tested, assuring perfect results every time.

Whether you consider yourself a gourmet or a beginning cook we're sure that our books will soon become a well-used collection on your shelf. In *Slow Cooker and Family Recipes*, you'll find a diverse and delicious range of 130 recipes. We've put together our favorite dishes, from classics such as *Traditional Pot Roast* and *Chicken Stew* to more exotic recipes such as *Sea Bass with Lemon Sauce*. In addition to the main dishes, you'll find a selection of appetizers and snacks, and dozens of salads and side dishes.

So what's more to say than here's to enjoying less time in the kitchen and more time with the family.

Happy Cooking and warmest wishes from all of us at

Blueberry Hill

Pantry Essentials

A well-stocked pantry helps to make life a little easier when trying to plan out what to cook. The ingredients listed below are the things you'll regularly find on our shopping list.

Dry Ingredients

Pasta Spaghetti and macaroni are good basic pastas but for a broader choice add lasagna (sheets), Cannelloni (tubes), fusilli (spirals), farfalle (bows), tagliatelle (ribbons) and conchiglie (shells).

Rice Every pantry should have a good long-grain rice supplemented with basmati rice, risotto rice and brown rice.

Noodles Most noodles are associated with Asian cooking. Make sure you have a selection of both Egg noodles and rice noodles for use in soups and stir-fries.

Flour All-purpose flour is great for thickening casseroles, making sauces and coating food before cooking. Self-rising flour is used for baking whilst bread making generally requires specific bread flour due to higher gluten levels.

Sugar White and brown sugar cover off the basic needs, but some recipes will call for confectioner's sugar for making frostings and for decoration.

Nuts and Seeds Walnuts, almonds, pine nuts and cashews can be used to add extra crunch and texture to savory dishes and baked goods. Make sure to store them in airtight containers. Sesame seeds are useful for many Asian inspired dishes.

Oils & Vinegars

Extra Virgin Olive Oil Ideal for drizzling over salads Extra Virgin Olive Oil is produced from the first cold-pressing of the olives and is a premium olive oil with a peppery, fruity flavor.

Vegetable Oil Made of a blend of various oils this is best used for frying, as it is very greasy.

Peanut Oil Suitable for drizzling, dressings and mayonnaise as well as forms of cooking this is a very versatile oil.

Wine Vinegars Available in many different varieties, mainly red, white and sherry. They can be used for dressings, marinades, and sauces or sprinkled over foods.

Balsamic Vinegar This delicious vinegar is thick, dark and slightly sweet. It is made from grape juice that is aged in barrels over a number of years.

Herbs & Spices

Nothing beats fresh herbs or spices but it's always good to have the following dried herbs and spices to hand.

Chili Powder This powdered mixture of spices includes dried chiles, cumin, coriander and cloves. Use it to flavor soups and stews.

Paprika This spice is made from ground sweet red pepper pods and its flavor can vary from mild, sweet and pungent to fiery hot. It is excellent in salad and as a garnish.

Bay Leaves Originally from the Mediterranean dried bay leaves add a good pungent flavor to soups, sauces and casseroles. They are usually discarded once the food has absorbed their flavor.

Chives Relatives of the onion family these herbs can be added to salads, soups, cream cheese and egg dishes.

Garlic A must for any kitchen fresh cloves of garlic store well or you can buy jars of garlic cloves or dried garlic for your dishes.

Thyme A very versatile herb that can be used with meat, poultry, egg and potato dishes and is also good in soups, sauces, roasts, casseroles and stews.

Five Spice Chinese five spice seasoning is a blend of cloves, cinnamon, fennel seeds, Sichuan peppercorns and Star Anise. It is very popular in stir-fries.

Ginger Dried ginger is particularly good with fruit, cookies and condiments.

Apple Pie Spice This blend of spices usually consists of cinnamon, nutmeg and cardamom. It has a warm, sweet flavor and is delicious in fruit desserts, bread, cakes cookies, pies and drinks.

Other Items

Bouillon Cubes Great for use in casseroles and soups if you do not have time to make or buy fresh stock.

Tomato Paste This is a condensed puree, which adds a more intense flavor in sauces and soups.

Canned Tomatoes Always useful for a variety of dishes, from sauces and soups to stews and casseroles.

Canned Beans Always have a few cans of beans to hand from Red kidney beans, to lentils and chickpeas. They don't require soaking and can be very useful to have in any pantry.

Canned Fish Many dishes can use canned or fresh fish. Tuna, crab and anchovies are all useful for salads or pasta dishes.

Pickled Foods Pickles, pickled onions and capers make perfect accompaniments and garnishes for meat and vegetable dishes.

Olives It's always useful to have a can or a bottle of olives. They are delicious in salads, pastas and on pizzas or to blend and make dips from.

Soy Sauce A popular Chinese sauce it is used within all Asian foods and adds a salty flavor. Soy comes in light and dark varieties use the light one with shellfish and the dark one with duck and meat.

Worcestershire Sauce This spicy sauce adds a fantastic fiery flavor to casseroles and soups.

Appetizers & Snacks

Shrimp Cocktail

2 pounds jumbo shrimp (12 to 15 per pound), deveined, but unpeeled

1 lemon cut in wedges

1 cup prepared cocktail sauce

For the poaching liquid

3 quarts cold water

½ onion, sliced

2 garlic cloves, peeled and bruised

2 springs tarragon

1 bay leaf

1 tablespoon Old Bay seasoning

½ lemon, juiced

1 teaspoon black peppercorns

For the cocktail sauce

½ cup ketchup

¼ cup chili sauce

¼ cup horseradish, or to taste

1 teaspoon fresh lemon juice

1 teaspoon Worcestershire sauce

Dash of hot sauce, optional

Pinch of salt

Frozen shrimp are now commonly available deveined (meaning the intestinal track removed), but with the shell on. This style makes the best shrimp cocktail since the shell adds flavor when they are poached.

If you can't find this type, get shell-on shrimp and use a pair of scissors to make a cut through the shell, down the back of the shrimp. Then use a small sharp knife to make ⅛ inch deep incision and remove the intestinal track. Rinse under cold water.

Add all the poaching liquid ingredients to a large stockpot. Place over high heat and bring to a simmer. Turn the heat down to low and simmer for 30 minutes.

Fill a mixing bowl with ice water and set aside. Turn the heat under the poaching liquid to high, and bring to a boil. Add the shrimp and boil for 5 minutes or until cooked through. Transfer the shrimp into the ice water. When cold, drain well, and serve with cocktail sauce and lemon wedges.

The shrimp can be served as is (also known as "peel and eat"), or for a "fancier" presentation, peel for your guests ahead of time and arrange around the rim of a cocktail glass.

For the sauce (makes 1 cup): Combine all ingredients in a small bowl, mix thoroughly, and refrigerate for at least one hour before serving.

Maryland Crab Cakes with Tartar Sauce

makes 6

1 large egg, beaten

2 tablespoons mayonnaise

½ teaspoon Dijon mustard

¼ teaspoon Worcestershire sauce

½ teaspoon Old Bay seasoning

¼ teaspoon salt

Pinch of cayenne pepper

1 pound fresh lump crabmeat, well drained

10 saltine crackers

Plain breadcrumbs

1 tablespoon vegetable oil

2 tablespoons unsalted butter

For the tartar sauce

1 cup mayonnaise

¼ cup sweet pickle relish

1 tablespoon finely minced onion

1 tablespoon chopped capers

1 tablespoon chopped parsley

1½ tablespoons freshly squeezed lemon juice

Dash of Worcestershire sauce

Few drops of Tabasco

Salt and pepper

Whisk together the egg, mayonnaise, mustard, Worcestershire, Old Bay, salt, and cayenne to a mixing bowl. Crush the crackers into very fine crumbs and add to the bowl. Stir until combined. Let sit for 5 minutes.

Gently fold in the crabmeat. Cover the bowl and refrigerate for at least 1 hour.

Sprinkle the breadcrumbs lightly over a large plate. Shape the crab mixture into 6 cakes, and place on the plate. Dust the tops of each crab cake lightly with more breadcrumbs. These cakes are almost all crab, which makes them fragile. They will bind together as the egg cooks, and golden-brown crust forms.

Heat the vegetable oil and butter in a large skillet over medium-high heat. When the foam from the butter begins to dissipate, carefully transfer each crab cake to the pan. Sauté until golden brown, about 4 minutes per side. Drain on a paper towel, and serve with the sauce.

For the sauce: Mix together all the ingredients in a bowl. Refrigerate at least an hour before serving. Makes 1½ cups.

Vegetarian Spring Rolls

serves 4

2 ounces fine cellophane noodles

2 tablespoons peanut oil

2 garlic cloves, crushed

½ teaspoon grated fresh gingerroot

⅔ cup oyster mushrooms, thinly sliced

2 scallions, finely chopped

½ cup bean sprouts

1 small carrot, finely shredded

½ teaspoon sesame oil

1 tablespoon light soy sauce

1 tablespoon rice wine or dry sherry

¼ teaspoon ground pepper

1 tablespoon chopped fresh cilantro

1 tablespoon chopped fresh mint

24 spring-roll wrappers

½ teaspoon cornstarch

Peanut oil, for deep frying

Place the noodles in a heatproof bowl, pour over enough boiling water to cover, and let stand for 4 minutes. Drain, rinse in cold water, then drain again. Cut into 2-inch lengths.

Heat the peanut oil in a wok or wide pan over high heat. Add the garlic, ginger, oyster mushrooms, scallions, bean sprouts, and carrot and stir-fry for about 1 minute until just soft.

Stir in the sesame oil, soy sauce, rice wine, pepper, cilantro, and mint, then remove from the heat. Stir in the rice noodles.

Arrange the spring-roll wrappers on a counter, pointing diagonally. Mix the cornstarch with 1 tablespoon water and brush the edges of 1 wrapper with this. Spoon a little filling onto one pointed side of a wrapper.

Roll the point of the wrapper over the filling, then fold the side points inward over the filling. Continue to roll up the wrapper away from you, moistening the tip with more cornstarch mixture to secure to the roll.

Heat the oil in a wok or deep pan to 350°F, or until a cube of bread browns in 30 seconds. Add rolls in batches and deep-fry for 2–3 minutes each until golden brown and crisp. Serve hot.

Sweet-and-Sour Chicken Wings

serves 4-6

1 pound 4 ounce chicken wings, tips removed

2 celery stalks, chopped

3 cups boiling chicken stock

2 tablespoons cornstarch

3 tablespoons white wine vinegar or rice vinegar

3 tablespoons dark soy sauce

5 tablespoons sweet chili sauce

¼ cup brown sugar

One 15-ounce can pineapple chunks in juice, drained

1 cup bamboo shoots

½ green bell pepper, seeded and thinly sliced

½ red bell pepper, seeded and thinly sliced

Salt

Put the chicken wings and celery in the slow cooker and season with salt. Pour in the chicken stock, cover, and cook on low for 5 hours.

Drain the chicken wings, reserving 1½ cups of the stock, and keep warm. Pour the reserved stock into a pan and stir in the cornstarch. Add the vinegar, soy sauce, and chili sauce. Place over a medium heat and stir in the sugar. Cook, stirring constantly, for 5 minutes, or until the sugar has dissolved completely and the sauce is thickened and smooth.

Lower the heat, stir in the pineapple, bamboo shoots, and bell peppers and simmer gently for 2–3 minutes. Stir in the chicken wings until they are thoroughly coated, then transfer to a serving platter.

Lamb & Rice Soup

serves 6

2 pounds 4 ounces boned leg of lamb, cut into 1-inch cubes

2 lamb bones, cracked

3 garlic cloves, peeled

8¾ cups water

½ cup long-grain rice

6 slices French bread

2 tablespoons chopped fresh parsley

Salt and pepper

Put the lamb, lamb bones, and garlic cloves into a large pan and pour in the water. Season well with salt and pepper and bring to a boil, skimming off any foam that rises to the surface. Transfer the mixture to the slow cooker, cover, and cook on low for 5 hours.

Meanwhile, soak the rice in several changes of cold water for 30 minutes, then drain.

Remove and discard the lamb bones and garlic cloves from the slow cooker, then stir in the rice. Re-cover and cook on low for an additional 2–2½ hours, until the lamb and rice are tender.

Shortly before serving, preheat the broiler. Place the bread slices on the broiler rack and lightly broil on both sides. Put 1 piece of bread into each individual serving bowl. Ladle the soup over the bread, sprinkle with the parsley, and serve immediately.

Philly Cheesesteak Sandwiches

serves 4

1 French baguette

12 ounces boneless rib-eye steak

3 tablespoons olive oil

1 onion, thinly sliced

1 green bell pepper, cored, seeded, and thinly sliced

½ cup fresh buffalo mozzarella, thinly sliced

Salt and pepper

Hot pepper sauce, for serving

Cut the baguette into 4 equal lengths, then cut each piece in half horizontally. Thinly slice the steak across its grain.

Heat 2 tablespoons of the oil in a large skillet over medium heat, add the onion and bell pepper, and cook, stirring occasionally, for 10–15 minutes until both vegetables are softened and the onion is golden brown. Push the mixture to one side of the skillet.

Heat the remaining oil in the skillet over medium heat. When hot, add the steak and stir-fry for 4–5 minutes until tender. Stir the onion mixture and steak together and season with salt and pepper.

Preheat the broiler to medium. Divide the steak mixture between the 4 bottom halves of bread and top with the cheese. Place them on a broiler rack and broil for 1–2 minutes until the cheese has melted, then cover with the top halves of bread and press down gently. Serve immediately with the hot pepper sauce.

Hummus with Vegetables

serves 4

1 cup canned chickpeas

4 tablespoons sesame seed paste

2 garlic cloves

½ cup lemon juice

2–3 tablespoons water

1 tablespoon olive oil

1 tablespoon chopped fresh parsley

pinch of cayenne

Pepper

Salt

Crudités

4 carrots

4 celery stalks

4 radishes

½ small cauliflower

1 green bell pepper, seeded

1 red bell pepper, seeded

Drain and rinse the chickpeas. Cut the carrots and celery into thin batons, cut the cauliflower into small florets, and cut the bell peppers into thin batons.

Place the chickpeas, sesame seed paste, garlic, and lemon juice in a blender or food processor and season to taste.

Process the ingredients, gradually adding water to the mixture as necessary until the consistency becomes smooth and creamy. Taste, and adjust the seasoning if necessary.

Transfer the mixture into a serving bowl and make a hollow in the center with the back of a spoon. Pour the olive oil into the hollow, then sprinkle the hummus with the chopped parsley and cayenne pepper.

Arrange the prepared crudités on a large serving platter and serve immediately with the hummus.

Clams Casino

18 medium-sized (about 2½ inches) of littleneck clams

2 tablespoons unsalted butter

3 strips center-cut bacon, each sliced into 6 equal pieces

3 tablespoons finely diced red bell pepper

3 garlic cloves, finely minced

⅓ cup plain breadcrumbs

1 tablespoon finely grated Parmesan

Pinch freshly ground black pepper

Pinch of salt

2 tablespoons chopped flat leaf parsley

Lemon wedges

Rock salt as needed

Shopping List:

Heat butter in a skillet over medium heat. Add the bacon and sauté until cooked, but not quite crisp. Using a slotted spoon, transfer the bacon to a plate and reserve.

Add the red pepper to the bacon drippings in the skillet, and cook for 2 minutes. Add the garlic and cook for 1 minute more. Turn off the heat and stir in the breadcrumbs, Parmesan, black pepper, and salt. Reserve the mixture until needed.

Add about 2 inches of water to a Dutch oven, or other heavy pot with a tight-fitting lid, and bring to a rapid boil over high heat. Add clams, cover, and cook for about 5 minutes, or just until the shells open. It's critical to remove and drain the clams as soon as they open. Allow the clams to cool until they can be handled.

Twist and pull the clamshells apart, and remove the clam. Place the clam back into the deeper of the two shell halves. Spread the rock salt on a heatproof baking dish, and set the clams on top of the salt, pressing in slightly.

Divide the breadcrumb mixture evenly over the top of each clamshell, and top with one piece of bacon. Broil on high, about 8 inches from the heat, until the tops are browned and the edges of the bacon are crisp. Sprinkle on the fresh parsley, and serve hot with lemon wedges.

Popovers

makes 4 popovers

2 tablespoons beef dripping or sunflower oil

1 cup all-purpose flour

½ teaspoon salt

2 extra-large eggs

1 cup whole milk

Preheat the oven to 425°F.

Grease six metal popover molds or six cups in a muffin pan with the dripping or sunflower oil. Divide the remaining dripping or oil equally between the molds or muffin pans.

Place into the pre-heated oven whilst you make the popovers.

Sift the flour and salt together into a large mixing bowl and make a well in the center. Break the eggs into the well, add the milk, and beat, gradually drawing in the flour from the side to make a smooth batter. Remove the molds from the oven and spoon in the batter until they are about halfway full.

Bake in the preheated oven for 30–35 minutes, without opening the door, until the popovers are well risen, puffed, and golden brown. Serve immediately.

Sweet Potato Patties

serves 4

1 pound sweet potatoes

2 garlic cloves, crushed

1 small fresh green chile, chopped

2 sprigs of fresh cilantro, chopped

1 tablespoon dark soy sauce

all-purpose flour, for shaping

vegetable oil, for frying

Sesame seeds, for sprinkling

Soy-tomato sauce

2 teaspoons vegetable oil

1 garlic clove, finely chopped

1½ teaspoons finely chopped fresh gingerroot

3 tomatoes, peeled and chopped

2 tablespoons dark soy sauce

1 tablespoon lime juice

2 tablespoons chopped fresh cilantro

To make the soy-tomato sauce, heat the oil in a wok and stir-fry the garlic and ginger for about 1 minute. Add the tomatoes and stir-fry for an additional 2 minutes. Remove from the heat and stir in the soy sauce, lime juice, and chopped cilantro. Set aside and keep warm.

Peel the sweet potatoes and grate finely (you can do this with a food processor). Place the garlic, chile, and cilantro in a mortar and crush to a smooth paste with a pestle. Stir in the soy sauce and mix with the sweet potatoes.

Divide the mixture into 12 equal portions. Dip into flour and pat into a flat, round patty shape.

Heat a shallow layer of oil in a wide skillet. Cook the sweet potato patties in batches over high heat until golden, turning once.

Drain on paper towels and sprinkle with the sesame seeds. Serve hot, with a spoonful of the soy-tomato sauce.

Onion & Mozzarella Tartlets

serves 4

1 pack (9-ounces) puff pastry, thawed, if frozen

2 medium red onions

1 red bell pepper

8 cherry tomatoes, halved

1 cup shredded mozzarella cheese

6-8 sprigs of fresh thyme

Preheat the broiler.

Roll out the pastry to make 4 x 3-inch squares. Using a sharp knife, trim the edges of the pastry, reserving the trimmings. Let the pastry chill in the refrigerator for 30 minutes.

Place the pastry squares on a baking sheet. Brush a little water along each edge of the pastry squares and use the reserved pastry trimmings to make a rim around each tartlet.

Cut the red onions into thin wedges and halve and seed the bell pepper.

Place the onions and bell pepper in a roasting pan. Cook under a preheated broiler for 15 minutes or until charred.

Place the roasted bell pepper halves in a plastic bag and let sweat for 10 minutes. Peel off the skin from the bell peppers and cut the flesh into strips.

Line the pastry squares with squares of foil. Bake in a preheated oven at 400°F for 10 minutes.

Place the onions, bell pepper strips, tomatoes, and cheese in each tartlet and sprinkle with the fresh thyme.

Return to the oven for 15 minutes or until the pastry is golden. Serve hot.

Crispy Chicken Fingers with Honey Mustard Dip

serves 8

1 cup all-purpose flour

2 teaspoons salt

1 teaspoon garlic salt

1 teaspoon chipotle pepper

½ teaspoon white pepper

4 large skinless, boneless chicken breasts, cut into ½-inch strips

4 eggs, beaten

1 tablespoon milk

3 cups Japanese-style panko bread crumbs

Vegetable oil for frying

For the dip

½ cup mayonnaise

2 tablespoons Dijon mustard

2 tablespoons yellow mustard

1 tablespoon rice vinegar

2 tablespoons honey

½ teaspoon hot sauce, optional

Combine the flour, salt, garlic salt, chipotle, and white pepper in a large, sealable plastic freezer bag. Shake to mix. Add the chicken strips, seal the bag, and shake vigorously to coat evenly.

In a mixing bowl, whisk together the eggs and milk. Add the chicken strips, shaking off the excess flour as you remove them from the bag. Stir until the strips are completely coated in the egg mixture.

Pour the breadcrumbs in a shallow pan. Use one hand (called the "wet" hand) to remove the chicken strips from the bowl of eggs, a few at a time, allowing the excess egg to drip off, and place in the pan of panko. Use the other hand (called the "dry" hand) to coat the chicken in the breadcrumbs, pressing them in firmly. As they are breaded, place the strips on baking sheets or racks. When done breading, let the chicken strips rest for 10 to 15 minutes before frying.

Pour about ½ inch of oil in a large, heavy skillet (ideally cast iron) and set over medium-high heat. When the oil is hot enough to fry (350°F to 375°F or test with a small piece of breading), cook for 2 to 3 minutes per side, or until golden brown and cooked through. Work in batches; drain on paper towels or baking racks, and keep the cooked chicken fingers in a warm oven (175°F) until all are done.

To make the honey mustard dip: Combine all the ingredients and mix well. Serve immediately.

Tomato & Lentil Soup

2 tablespoons vegetable oil

1 onion, chopped

1 garlic clove, finely chopped

2 celery stalks, chopped

2 carrots, chopped

1 teaspoon ground cumin

1 teaspoon ground coriander

¾ cup red or yellow lentils

1 tablespoon tomato paste

5 cups vegetable stock

One 14.5-ounce can chopped tomatoes

1 bay leaf

Salt and pepper

Sour cream and toasted crusty bread, to serve

Heat the oil in a pan. Add the onion and garlic and cook over low heat, stirring occasionally, for 5 minutes, until softened. Stir in the celery and carrots and cook, for an additional 4 minutes. Stir in the cumin and coriander and cook, stirring, for 1 minute, then add the lentils.

Mix the tomato paste with a little of the stock in a small bowl and add to the pan with the remaining stock, the tomatoes, and bay leaf. Bring to a boil, then transfer to the slow cooker. Stir well, cover, and cook on low for 3½–4 hours.

Remove and discard the bay leaf. Transfer the soup to a food processor or blender and process until smooth. Season to taste with salt and pepper. Ladle into warmed soup bowls, top each with a swirl of sour cream, and serve immediately with toasted crusty bread.

Deep-fried Chili Corn Balls

serves 4

6 scallions, sliced

3 tablespoons chopped fresh cilantro

1 cup canned corn

1 teaspoon mild chili powder

1 tablespoon sweet chili sauce

¼ cup shredded coconut

1 egg

⅓ cup cornmeal

Oil, for deep-frying

Extra sweet chili sauce, for serving

In a large bowl, mix together the scallions, cilantro, corn, chili powder, chili sauce, coconut, egg, and cornmeal until well blended.

Cover the bowl with plastic wrap and let stand for about 10 minutes.

Heat the oil for deep-frying in a large preheated wok or skillet to 350°F or until a cube of bread browns in 30 seconds.

Carefully drop spoonfuls of the chili and cornmeal mixture into the hot oil. Deep-fry the chili corn balls, in batches, for 4–5 minutes or until crispy and a deep golden brown color.

Remove the chili corn balls with a slotted spoon, transfer to paper towels, and let drain thoroughly.

Transfer the chili corn balls to serving plates and serve with extra sweet chili sauce, for dipping.

Carrot & Coriander Soup

1 tablespoon butter

1½ tablespoons sunflower oil

1 yellow onion, finely chopped

4 large carrots, diced

½-inch piece fresh ginger

2 teaspoons ground coriander

1 teaspoon all-purpose flour

5 cups vegetable stock

⅔ cup sour cream

2 tablespoons chopped fresh cilantro

Salt and pepper

Croutons, to serve

Melt the butter with the oil in a pan. Add the onion, carrots, and ginger, cover, and cook over low heat, stirring occasionally, for 8 minutes, until softened and just beginning to color.

Sprinkle over the ground coriander and flour and cook, stirring constantly, for 1 minute. Gradually stir in the stock, a little at a time, and bring to a boil, stirring constantly. Season to taste with salt and pepper.

Transfer the mixture to the slow cooker, cover, and cook on low for 4–5 hours. Ladle the soup into a food processor or blender, in batches if necessary, and process until smooth. Return the soup to the slow cooker and stir in the sour cream. Cover and cook on low for an additional 15–20 minutes, until heated through.

Ladle the soup into warmed soup bowls, sprinkle with the chopped cilantro, and top with croutons. Serve immediately.

Tuna Melts

4 slices sourdough bread

Two 5-ounce cans tuna in oil, drained and flaked

4 tablespoons mayonnaise, or to taste

1 tablespoon Dijon mustard or whole grain mustard, plus extra, to taste

4 scallions, trimmed and chopped

2 tablespoons finely chopped dill pickle or sweet pickle, to taste

1 hard-cooked egg, shelled and finely chopped

1 small carrot, grated

1 tablespoon rinsed and coarsely chopped capers in brine

2 tablespoons chopped parsley or chives

4 large lettuce leaves, such as romaine

8 thin slices cheddar cheese

Salt and pepper

Preheat the broiler to high and position the broiler rack about 4 inches from the heat source.

Line a baking sheet with foil and set aside.

Toast the bread under the preheated broiler for 2 minutes on each side, or until crisp and lightly browned.

Meanwhile, put the tuna in a bowl with the mayonnaise and mustard and beat together to break up the tuna.
Add the scallions, pickle, egg, carrot, capers, and salt and pepper to taste and beat together, adding extra mayonnaise to taste. Stir in the parsley.

Put the toast on the foil-lined baking sheet and top each slice with a lettuce leaf. Divide the tuna salad among the slices of toast and spread out. Top each sandwich with cheese slices, cut to fit.

Place under the broiler and broil for 2 minutes, or until the cheese is melted and lightly browned.

Cut each tuna melt into four slices, transfer to a plate, and serve immediately.

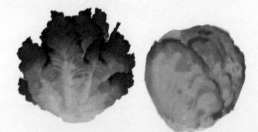

Tex-Mex Bean Dip

serves 4

2 tablespoons corn oil

1 onion, finely chopped

2 garlic cloves, finely chopped

2–3 fresh green chiles, seeded and finely chopped

One 15-ounce can refried beans or red kidney beans

2 tablespoons chili sauce

6 tablespoons hot vegetable stock

1 cup Cheddar cheese, grated

Salt and pepper

1 fresh red chile, seeded and shredded, to garnish

Tortilla chips, to serve

Heat the oil in a large, heavy skillet. Add the onion, garlic, and chiles and cook, stirring occasionally, over low heat for 5 minutes until the onion is soft and translucent. Transfer the mixture to the slow cooker.

Add the refried beans to the slow cooker. If using red kidney beans, drain well and rinse under cold running water. Reserve 2 tablespoons of the beans and mash the remainder coarsely with a potato masher. Add all the beans to the slow cooker.

Add the sauce, hot stock, and grated cheese, season with salt and pepper, and stir well. Cover and cook on low for 2 hours.

Transfer the dip to a serving bowl, garnish with shredded red chile, and serve warm with tortilla chips on the side.

CERTIFIED ORGANIC

Valley Farm

Red Kidney Beans

nt.wt. 12oz

Oyster Rockefeller

serves 4

24 large live oysters

Rock salt

3 tablespoons butter

6 scallions, chopped

1 large garlic clove, crushed

3 tablespoons finely chopped celery

1½ ounces watercress sprigs

1¾ cups young spinach leaves, rinsed and any tough stems removed

1 tablespoon anise-flavored liqueur, such as Anisette or Pastis

4 tablespoons fresh bread crumbs

Few drops of hot pepper sauce, to taste

Salt and pepper

Lemon wedges, to serve

Pre-heat oven to 400°F.

Shuck the oysters, running an oyster knife under each oyster to loosen it from its shell. Pour off the liquor. Arrange a ½ to ¾ inch layer of salt in a roasting pan large enough to hold the oysters in a single layer, or use 2 roasting pans. Nestle the oyster shells in the salt so that they remain upright. Cover with a thick, damp dish towel and let chill while you make the topping.

If you don't have oyster plates with indentations that hold the shells upright, line 4 plates with a layer of salt deep enough to hold six shells upright. Set the plates aside.

Melt half the butter in a large skillet over medium heat. Add the scallions, garlic, and celery and cook, stirring frequently, for 2 to 3 minutes until softened.

Stir in the remaining butter, then add the watercress and spinach and cook, stirring constantly, for 1 minute, or until the leaves wilt. Transfer to a blender or small food processor and add the liqueur, bread crumbs, hot pepper sauce, and salt and pepper to taste. Whiz until well blended.

Spoon 2 to 3 teaspoons of the sauce over each oyster. Bake in the oven for 20 minutes. Transfer to the prepared plates and serve with lemon wedges.

Sticky Ginger Garlic Wings

makes 40

4 pounds chicken wings

1 tablespoon vegetable oil

1 tablespoon all-purpose flour

1 teaspoon salt

For the Sticky Ginger Garlic Sauce

4 crushed garlic cloves, peeled, finely minced

2 tablespoons freshly grated ginger root

¼ teaspoon hot pepper flakes, or to taste

½ cup rice vinegar

½ cup packed dark brown sugar

1 teaspoon soy sauce

Pre-heat oven to 425°F.

If the chicken wings being used were frozen and thawed, be sure they're completely dry before starting recipe. If using whole wings, cut each into two pieces (in wing-speak called the "flat" and the "drum"). The small wing tips can be discarded, or saved for stock. In a large mixing bowl, toss the wings with the oil and salt. Add the flour and toss until evenly coated.

Line two heavy-duty baking sheets with lightly greased foil, or silicon baking mats. Divide the wings and spread out evenly. Do not crowd. Bake for 25 minutes, remove, and turn the wings over. Return to the oven and cook another 2 0 to 30 minutes, or until the wings are well-browned and cooked through.

Note: Cooking times will vary based on size of the wings. When fully cooked, the bones will easily pull out from the meat.

While the wings are baking, mix all the sauce ingredients in a saucepan. Bring to a simmer, whisking, over medium heat. Remove from heat and reserve.

After the wings are cooked, transfer to a large mixing bowl. Pour the warm sauce over the hot wings and toss with a spoon or spatula to completely coat. Let rest 10 minutes, and toss again. The glaze will get sticky and thicken slightly as is cools. Serve warm or room temperature.

Spinach & Herb Frittata

serves 6-8

4 tablespoons olive oil

6 scallions, sliced

9 ounces young spinach leaves, coarse stems removed, rinsed

6 large eggs

3 tablespoons finely chopped mixed fresh herbs

2 tablespoons freshly grated Parmesan cheese, plus extra for garnish

Salt and pepper

Fresh parsley, for garnish

Heat a 10-inch nonstick skillet with a flameproof handle over medium heat. Add the oil and heat. Add the scallions and cook for about 2 minutes.

Add the spinach and cook until it just wilts. Beat the eggs in a large bowl and season with salt and pepper to taste. Using a slotted spoon, transfer the spinach and scallions to the bowl of eggs and stir in the herbs. Pour the excess oil into a heatproof pitcher, then scrape off the crusty sediment from the bottom of the skillet.

Reheat the skillet. Add 2 tablespoons of the reserved oil. Pour in the egg mixture, smoothing it into an even layer. Cook, shaking the skillet occasionally, for 6 minutes or until the base is set when you lift up the side with a spatula.

Sprinkle the top of the frittata with the Parmesan cheese. Place the skillet under a preheated broiler and cook for 3 minutes or until the excess liquid is set and the cheese is golden.

Remove the skillet from the heat and slide the frittata onto a serving plate. Let stand for at least 5 minutes before cutting and garnishing with extra Parmesan cheese and parsley. Serve hot or at room temperature.

Warm Garbanzo Bean Salad

serves 6

1 cup dried garbanzo beans, soaked overnight or for at least 5 hours

1 cup pitted black olives

4 scallions, finely chopped fresh parsley sprigs, to garnish

Crusty bread, to serve

For the dressing

2 tablespoons red wine vinegar

2 tablespoons mixed chopped fresh herbs, such as parsley, rosemary, and thyme

3 garlic cloves, very finely chopped

½ cup extra virgin olive oil

Salt and pepper

Drain and rinse the beans, place in a saucepan, cover with fresh cold water, and bring to a boil. Boil rapidly for at least 10 minutes, then remove from the heat, drain and rinse again. Place the beans in the slow cooker and add fresh cold water to cover. Cover and cook on low for 12 hours.

Drain well and transfer to a bowl. Stir in the olives and scallions.

To make the dressing, whisk together the vinegar, herbs, and garlic in a pitcher, and season with salt and pepper to taste. Gradually whisk in the olive oil.

Pour the dressing over the still-warm garbanzos and toss lightly to coat. Garnish with the parsley sprigs and serve warm with crusty bread.

Bean & Vegetable Soup

serves 4-6

2¾ cups dried navy beans, soaked overnight or for at least 5 hours

2 onions, finely chopped

2 garlic cloves, finely chopped

2 potatoes, chopped

2 carrots, chopped

2 tomatoes, peeled and chopped

2 celery stalks, chopped

4 tablespoon extra virgin olive oil

1 bay leaf

Salt and pepper

To garnish

12 black olives

2 tablespoon chopped fresh chives

Drain and rinse the beans, place in a saucepan, cover with fresh cold water, and bring to a boil. Boil rapidly for at least 10 minutes, then remove from the heat, drain and rinse again. Place them in the slow cooker and add the onions, garlic, potatoes, carrots, tomatoes, celery, olive oil, and bay leaf.

Pour in 8¾ cups boiling water, making sure that all the ingredients are fully submerged. Cover and cook on low for 12 hours until the beans are tender.

Remove and discard the bay leaf. Season the soup to taste with salt and pepper, and stir in the olives and chives.

Ladle into warmed soup bowls and serve.

Warm Crab Dip

serves 8-11

1 ¾ cups cream cheese

¾ cup cheddar cheese, grated

1 cup sour cream

4 tablespoons mayonnaise

2 tablespoons lemon juice

2 teaspoons Dijon mustard

2 teaspoons Worcestershire sauce, plus extra to taste

1 pound 2 ounces cooked fresh crabmeat

1 garlic clove, halved

Salt and pepper

Butter, for greasing

Sprigs of fresh dill, for garnish

Savory crackers, for serving

Put the cream cheese into a bowl and stir in the cheese, sour cream, mayonnaise, lemon juice, mustard, and Worcestershire sauce.

Add the crabmeat and salt and pepper to taste and gently stir together. Taste and add extra Worcestershire sauce, if desired. Cover and let chill for 24 hours.

When you are ready to heat the dip, remove it from the refrigerator and let it come to room temperature.

Meanwhile, preheat the oven to 350°F. Rub the cut sides of the garlic clove over the base and sides of an ovenproof dish suitable for serving from, then lightly grease.

Spoon the crab mixture into the dish and smooth the surface. Heat the dip through in the oven for 15 minutes.

Buffalo Chicken Wings

makes 40

4 pounds chicken wings

1 tablespoon vegetable oil

1 tablespoon all-purpose flour

1 teapoon salt

For the sauce

⅔ cup Frank's Louisiana hot sauce

1 stick (½ cup) cold unsalted butter, cut into 1 inch slices

1½ tablespoons white vinegar

¼ teaspoon Worcestershire sauce

1 teaspoon Tabasco

¼ teaspoon cayenne pepper

Pinch garlic powder

Salt to taste

Pre-heat oven to 425°F.

If the chicken wings being used were frozen and thawed, be sure they're completely dry before starting recipe. If using whole wings, cut each into two pieces (in wing-speak called the "flat" and the "drum"). The small wing tips can be discarded, or saved for stock. In a large mixing bowl, toss the wings with the oil, salt, and flour until evenly coated

Line two heavy-duty baking sheets with lightly greased foil, or silicon baking mats. Divide the wings and spread out evenly. Do not crowd. Bake for 25 minutes, remove, and turn the wings over. Return to the oven and cook another 20 to 30 minutes, or until the wings are well-browned and cooked through

Note: Cooking times will vary based on size of the wings. When fully cooked, the bones will easily pull out from the meat.

While the wings are baking, mix all the sauce ingredients in a saucepan. Bring to a simmer, whisking, over medium heat. Remove from heat and reserve. Taste sauce; adjust for salt and spiciness, if desired.

After the wings are cooked, transfer to a large mixing bowl. Pour the warm sauce over the hot wings and toss with a spoon or spatula to completely coat. Let rest 5 minutes, toss again, and serve immediately with celery sticks and blue cheese dressing on the side.

Bacon & Lentil Soup

serves 4

1 pound thick, rindless smoked bacon strips, diced

1 onion, chopped

2 carrots, sliced

2 celery stalks, chopped

1 turnip, chopped

1 large potato, chopped

½ cup green lentils

4 cups chicken stock or water

Salt and pepper

1 tablespoon dried mixed herbs

Heat a large, heavy pan. Add the bacon and cook over low heat, stirring frequently, for 4–5 minutes, until the fat runs. Add the onion, carrots, celery, turnip, and potato and cook, stirring frequently, for 5 minutes.

Add the lentils and mixed herbs and pour in the stock. Bring to a boil, then transfer the mixture to the slow cooker. Cover and cook on low for 8–9 hours, or until the lentils are tender.

Season the soup to taste with pepper and salt, if necessary. Ladle into warmed soup bowls and serve.

Chicken Satay Skewers with Peanut Sauce

serves 4

4 skinless, boneless chicken breasts, about 4 ounces each, cut into ¾-inch cubes

4 tablespoons soy sauce

1 tablespoon cornstarch

2 garlic cloves, finely chopped

1-inch piece fresh ginger, peeled and finely chopped

¼ cucumber, coarsely chopped, to serve

Peanut sauce

2 tablespoons peanut or vegetable oil

½ onion, finely chopped

1 garlic clove, finely chopped

4 tablespoons chunky peanut butter

4–5 tablespoons water

½ teaspoon chili powder

Put the chicken cubes in a shallow dish. Mix the soy sauce, cornstarch, garlic, and ginger together in a small bowl and pour over the chicken. Cover and let marinate in the refrigerator for at least 2 hours.

Meanwhile, soak 12 bamboo skewers in cold water for at least 30 minutes. Preheat the broiler. Thread the chicken pieces onto the bamboo skewers. Transfer the skewers to a broiler pan and cook under the preheated broiler for 3–4 minutes. Turn the skewers over and cook for an additional 3–4 minutes, or until cooked through.

Meanwhile, to make the sauce, heat the oil in a saucepan, add the onion and garlic, and cook over medium heat, stirring frequently, for 3–4 minutes until softened. Add the peanut butter, water, and chili powder and simmer for 2–3 minutes, until softened and thinned. Serve the skewers immediately with the warm sauce and cucumber.

Slow Cooker
Favorites

Tagliatelle with Meat Sauce

serves 6

3 tablespoons olive oil

3 slices bacon, chopped

1 onion, chopped

1 garlic clove, finely chopped

1 carrot, chopped

1 celery stalk, chopped

1 pound ground beef

½ cup red wine

2 tablespoons tomato paste

One 14.5-ounce can chopped tomatoes

1¼ cups beef stock

½ teaspoon dried oregano

1 bay leaf

1 pound dried tagliatelle

Salt and pepper

Grated Parmesan cheese, to serve

Heat the oil in a pan. Add the bacon and cook over medium heat, stirring frequently, for 3 minutes. Reduce the heat, add the onion, garlic, carrot, and celery and cook, stirring occasionally, for 5 minutes, until the vegetables have softened.

Increase the heat to medium and add the ground beef. Cook, stirring frequently and breaking it up with a wooden spoon, for 8–10 minutes, until evenly browned. Pour in the wine and cook for a few minutes, until the alcohol has evaporated, then stir in the tomato paste, tomatoes, stock, oregano, and bay leaf and season to taste with salt and pepper.

Bring to a boil, then transfer to the slow cooker. Cover and cook on low for 8–8 ½ hours.

Shortly before serving, bring a large pan of lightly salted water to a boil. Add the pasta, bring back to a boil, and cook for 8–10 minutes, until tender but still firm to the bite. Drain and put into a warmed serving bowl. Remove and discard the bay leaf, then add the meat sauce to the pasta. Toss with 2 forks, sprinkle with the Parmesan , and serve immediately.

Ham with Black-eyed Peas

serves 4

1¼ pounds country-cured ham

2–3 tablespoons olive oil

1 onion, chopped

2–3 garlic cloves, chopped

2 celery ribs, chopped

1-2 carrots, thinly sliced

1 cinnamon stick

½ teaspoon ground cloves

¼ teaspoon freshly grated nutmeg

1 teaspoon dried oregano

2 cups chicken or vegetable broth

2 tablespoons maple syrup

8 ounces chorizo or other spicy sausages, skinned

One 15-ounce can black-eyed peas, drained and rinsed

1 orange bell pepper, seeded and chopped

1 tablespoon cornstarch

Freshly ground black pepper

Fresh Italian parsley or oregano sprig, to garnish

Trim off any fat from the ham and cut the flesh into 1½-inch pieces. Heat 1 tablespoon of the oil in a heavy skillet, add the ham, and cook over high heat, stirring frequently, for 5 minutes, until browned all over. Using a slotted spoon, transfer the ham to the slow cooker.

Add 1 tablespoon of the remaining oil to the skillet. Reduce the heat to low, add the onion, garlic, celery, and carrots, and cook, stirring occasionally, for 5 minutes, until the vegetables have softened. Add the cinnamon, cloves, and nutmeg, season with pepper, and cook, stirring constantly, for 2 minutes. Stir in the dried oregano, broth, and maple syrup and bring to a boil, stirring constantly. Pour the mixture over the ham, stir well, cover, and cook on low for 5–6 hours.

Heat the remaining oil in a skillet, add the chorizo, and cook, turning frequently, for 10 minutes, until browned all over. Remove from the skillet, cut each sausage into 3–4 chunks, and add to the slow cooker with the black-eyed peas and bell pepper. Re-cover and cook on high for 1–1½ hours.

Stir the cornstarch with 2 tablespoons water to a smooth paste in a small bowl, then stir into the stew, re-cover, and cook on high for 15 minutes. Remove and discard the cinnamon stick, garnish the stew with a fresh herb sprig, and serve.

Goulash

4 tablespoons vegetable oil

1½ pounds chuck or other braising beef, cut into 1-inch cubes

2 teaspoons all-purpose flour

2 teaspoons paprika

1½ cups beef stock

3 onions, chopped

4 carrots, peeled and diced

1 large potato or 2 medium potatoes, diced

1 bay leaf

1 teaspoon caraway seeds

One 14.5-ounce can chopped tomatoes

2 tablespoons sour cream

Salt and freshly ground pepper, to taste

Heat 2 tablespoons of oil in a heavy skillet. Add the beef and cook over medium heat, stirring frequently, until browned all over. Lower the heat and stir in the flour and paprika. Cook, stirring constantly, for 2 minutes. Gradually stir in the stock and bring to a boil, then transfer the mixture to the slow cooker.

Rinse out the skillet and heat the remaining oil in it. Add the onions and cook over low heat, stirring occasionally, for 5 minutes until softened. Stir in the carrots and potato and cook for a few minutes more. Add the bay leaf, caraway seeds, and tomatoes with their can juices. Season to taste with salt and pepper.

Transfer the vegetable mixture to the slow cooker, stir well, then cover, and cook on low for 9 hours until the meat is tender.

Remove and discard the bay leaf. Pour the sour cream over the stew and serve immediately.

Easy Chinese Chicken

serves 4

2 teaspoons grated fresh ginger

4 garlic cloves, finely chopped

2 star anise

⅔ cup Chinese rice wine or medium dry sherry

2 tablespoons dark soy sauce

1 teaspoon sesame oil

5 tablespoons water

4 skinless chicken thighs or drumsticks shredded scallions, to garnish

Cooked rice, to serve

Combine the ginger, garlic, star anise, rice wine, soy sauce, sesame oil, and water in a bowl. Place the chicken in a pan, add the spice mixture, and bring to a boil.

Transfer to the slow cooker, cover, and cook on low for 4 hours, or until the chicken is tender and cooked through.

Remove and discard the star anise. Transfer the chicken to warmed plates, garnish with shredded scallions, and serve immediately with rice.

Summer Vegetable Casserole

serves 4

One 14.5-ounce can cannellini beans, drained and rinsed

One 15-ounce can artichoke hearts, drained

1 red bell pepper, seeded and sliced

4 small turnips, sliced

1 pound 6 ounces baby spinach leaves, coarse stalks removed

6 thyme sprigs

1¾ cups baby fava beans

1 tablespoon olive oil

2 tablespoons butter

4 shallots, chopped

4 leeks, sliced

3 celery stalks, sliced

3 tablespoons all-purpose flour

1 cup dry white wine

⅔ cup vegetable stock

Salt and pepper

Put the cannellini beans, artichoke hearts, bell pepper, turnips, spinach, and 4 of the thyme sprigs into the slow cooker.

Cook the fava beans in a small pan of lightly salted boiling water for 10 minutes.

Meanwhile, heat the oil and butter in a large skillet. Add the shallots, leeks, and celery and cook over low heat, stirring occasionally, for 5 minutes, until softened. Stir in the flour and cook, stirring constantly, for 1 minute. Gradually stir in the wine and stock and bring to a boil, stirring constantly. Season to taste with salt and pepper.

Transfer the contents of the skillet to the slow cooker. Drain the fava beans and add to the slow cooker. Stir well, cover, and cook on low for 2½–3 hours. Remove and discard the thyme sprigs. Sprinkle with the leaves from the remaining thyme sprigs and serve immediately.

Venison Casserole

3 tablespoons olive oil

2 pounds 4 ounces stewing venison, cut into 1¼-inch cubes

2 onions, thinly sliced

2 garlic cloves, chopped

1½ cups beef stock

2 tablespoons all-purpose flour

½ cup port

2 tablespoons red currant jelly

6 juniper berries, crushed

4 cloves, crushed

Pinch of ground cinnamon

Pinch of freshly grated nutmeg

Salt and pepper

Mashed potatoes, to serve

Heat the oil in a heavy skillet. Add the venison and cook over high heat, stirring frequently, for 5 minutes, until browned all over. Using a slotted spoon, transfer it to the slow cooker.

Add the onions and garlic to the skillet, lower the heat, and cook, stirring occasionally, for 5 minutes, until softened. Transfer them to the slow cooker.

Gradually stir the stock into the skillet, scraping up any sediment from the base, then bring to a boil, stirring constantly. Sprinkle the flour over the meat in the slow cooker and stir well to coat evenly. Stir in the hot stock, then stir in the port, red currant jelly, juniper berries, cloves, cinnamon, and nutmeg. Season with salt and pepper. Cover and cook on low for 7–8 hours, until the meat is tender.

Taste and adjust the seasoning if necessary. Remove and discard the cloves, then serve with mashed potatoes.

Chicken Cacciatore

serves 4

3 tablespoons olive oil

Four 6 ounce skinless chicken parts, such as breasts, thighs, or drumsticks

2 onions, sliced

2 garlic cloves, finely chopped

One 14.5-ounce can chopped tomatoes

1 tablespoon tomato paste

2 tablespoons chopped fresh parsley

2 teaspoons fresh thyme leaves

⅔ cup red wine

Salt and freshly ground pepper, to taste

Fresh thyme sprigs, to garnish

Heat the oil in a heavy skillet. Add the chicken portions and cook over medium heat, turning occasionally, for 10 minutes until golden all over. Using a slotted spoon, transfer the chicken to the slow cooker.

Add the onions to the skillet and cook, stirring occasionally, for 5 minutes until softened and just turning golden. Add the garlic, tomatoes and their can juices, tomato paste, parsley, thyme, and wine. Season to taste with salt and pepper and bring to a boil.

Pour the tomato mixture over the chicken pieces. Cover and cook on low for 5 hours until the chicken is tender and cooked through. Taste and adjust the seasoning if necessary, and serve, garnished with sprigs of thyme.

Pork & Beans

serves 4

2 tablespoons vegetable oil

4 pork chops, trimmed of excess fat

1 onion, chopped

One 14.5-ounce can chopped tomatoes

One 16-ounce can baked beans

Butter, for greasing, plus extra for browning (optional)

1 pound 9-ounces potatoes, thinly sliced

2 cups hot chicken stock

Salt and pepper

Heat the oil in a skillet. Season the chops well with salt and pepper, add to the skillet, and cook over medium heat for 2–3 minutes on each side, until evenly browned. Remove the skillet from the heat and transfer the chops to a plate.

Combine the onion, tomatoes, and baked beans in a bowl and season well with salt and pepper.

Lightly grease the slow cooker pot, then make a layer of half the potatoes in the bottom. Cover with half the tomato-and-bean mixture. Put the chops on top, then add the remaining tomato-and-bean mixture. Cover with the remaining potato slices. Pour in the stock, cover, and cook on low for 8–10 hours.

If desired, dot the topping with butter, then place the slow cooker pot under a preheated broiler to brown the potatoes before serving.

Caribbean Beef Stew

serves 6

1 pound braising beef

3 cups diced pumpkin or other squash

1 onion, chopped

1 red bell pepper, seeded and chopped

2 garlic cloves, finely chopped

1-inch piece fresh ginger, finely chopped

1 tablespoon sweet or hot paprika

1 cup beef stock

One 14.5-ounce can chopped tomatoes

One 10.5-ounce can chickpeas, drained and rinsed

One 10.5-ounce can black-eyed peas, drained and rinsed

Salt and pepper

Trim off any visible fat from the beef, then dice the meat. Heat a large heavy pan without adding any extra fat. Add the meat and cook, stirring constantly, for a few minutes, until evenly browned.

Stir in the pumpkin, onion, and bell pepper and cook for 1 minute, then add the garlic, ginger, and paprika. Pour in the stock, add the tomatoes, and bring to a boil.

Transfer the mixture to the slow cooker, cover, and cook on low for 7 hours. Add the chick peas and black-eyed peas to the stew and season to taste with salt and pepper.

Re-cover and cook on high for 30 minutes. Serve immediately.

Sea Bass in Lemon Sauce

serves 4

8 sea bass fillets

4 tablespoons unsalted butter

4 tablespoons all-purpose flour

3¾ cups warm milk

4 tablespoons lemon juice

3 cups sliced mushrooms

2 bay leaves

1 tablespoon dried mixed herbs

Salt and pepper

Lemon wedges and grilled asparagus, to serve

Put the fish fillets into the slow cooker and set aside.

Melt the butter in a pan over low heat. Add the flour and cook, stirring constantly, for 1 minute. Gradually stir in the milk, a little at a time, and bring to a boil, stirring constantly.

Stir in the lemon juice and mushrooms, add the dried mixed herbs and the bay leaf. Season to taste with salt and pepper. Reduce the heat and simmer for 5 minutes. Pour the sauce over the fish fillets, cover, and cook on low for 1½ hours.

Carefully lift out the fish fillets and put them on warmed individual plates. Remove and discard the bay leaf and spoon the sauce over the fish. Serve immediately with lemon wedges and asparagus.

Risotto with Spring Vegetables

5 cups vegetable stock

large pinch of saffron threads

4 tablespoons butter

1 tablespoon olive oil

1 onion, chopped

2 garlic cloves, finely chopped

1 cup risotto rice

3 tablespoons dry white wine

1 bay leaf

2½ cups mixed spring vegetables, such as asparagus spears, green beans, baby carrots, baby fava beans, and young green peas, thawed if frozen

2 tablespoons chopped fresh flat-leaf parsley

⅔ cup grated Parmesan cheese

Salt and pepper

Put a generous ⅓ cup of the stock into a small bowl, crumble in the saffron threads, and let steep. Reserve ⅔ cup of the remaining stock and heat the remainder in a pan.

Meanwhile, melt 2 tablespoons of the butter with the oil in a separate large pan. Add the onion and garlic and cook over low heat, stirring occasionally, for 5 minutes, until softened. Stir in the rice and cook, stirring constantly, for 1–2 minutes, until all the grains are coated and glistening. Pour in the wine and cook, stirring constantly, for a few minutes, until all the alcohol has evaporated. Season to taste with salt and pepper. Pour in the hot stock and the saffron mixture, add the bay leaf, and bring to a boil, stirring constantly.

Transfer the mixture to the slow cooker, cover, and cook on low for 2 hours. Meanwhile, if using fresh vegetables, slice the asparagus spears, green beans, and carrots and blanch all the vegetables in boiling water for 5 minutes. Drain and reserve.

Stir the reserved stock into the rice mixture, if it seems dry, and add the mixed vegetables, sprinkling them evenly over the top. Re-cover and cook on low for an additional 30–45 minutes, until heated through.

Remove and discard the bay leaf. Gently stir in the parsley, the remaining butter, and the Parmesan and serve immediately.

Sweet & Sour Pasta

serves 4

4 tablespoons olive oil

1 large red onion, sliced

2 garlic cloves, finely chopped

2 red bell peppers, seeded and sliced

2 zucchini, cut into sticks

1 eggplant, cut into sticks

2 cups strained pureed tomatoes

⅔ cup water

4 tablespoons lemon juice

2 tablespoons balsamic vinegar

½ cup sliced pitted black olives

1 tablespoon sugar

14 ounces dried pappardelle pasta

Salt and pepper

Fresh flat-leaf parsley leaves, to garnish

Heat the oil in a large heavy pan. Add the onion, garlic, and bell peppers and cook over low heat, stirring occasionally, for 5 minutes. Add the zucchini and eggplant and cook, stirring occasionally, for an additional 5 minutes. Stir in the strained pureed tomatoes and water and bring to a boil. Stir in the lemon juice, vinegar, olives, and sugar and season to taste with salt and pepper.

Transfer the mixture to the slow cooker. Cover and cook on low for 5 hours, until all the vegetables are tender.

Shortly before serving, bring a large pan of lightly salted water to a boil. Add the pasta, bring back to a boil, and cook for 8–10 minutes, until tender but still firm to the bite. Drain and transfer to a warmed serving dish, then spoon the vegetable mixture over the pasta and toss lightly. Garnish with parsley leaves and serve immediately.

Traditional Pot Roast

serves 6

1 onion, finely chopped

4 carrots, sliced

4 baby turnips sliced

4 celery stalks, sliced

2 potatoes, peeled and sliced

1 sweet potato, peeled and sliced

3–4 pounds beef pot roast

2 bay leaves

1 tablespoon dried mixed herbs

1¼ cups boiling beef stock

Salt and pepper

Place the onion, carrots, turnips, celery, potatoes, and sweet potato in the slow cooker and stir to mix well.

Rub the beef all over with salt and pepper, then place on top of the bed of vegetables. Add the bay leaves and the dried mixed herbs and pour in the stock. Cover and cook on low for 9–10 hours, until the beef is cooked to your liking.

Remove the beef, carve into slices, and arrange on serving plates. Spoon some of the vegetables and cooking juices onto the plates and serve.

Vegetable Curry

2 tablespoons vegetable oil

1 teaspoon cumin seeds

1 onion, sliced

2 curry leaves

1-inch piece fresh gingerroot, finely chopped

2 red chiles, seeded and chopped

2 tablespoons curry paste

2 carrots, sliced

1½ cups snow peas

1 head cauliflower, cut into florets

3 tomatoes, peeled and chopped

¾ cup frozen peas, thawed

½ teaspoon ground turmeric

Salt and freshly ground pepper, to taste

⅔–1 cup boiling vegetable or chicken broth

Heat the oil in a large, heavy pan. Add the cumin seeds and cook, stirring constantly, for 1–2 minutes until they give off their aroma and begin to pop. Add the onion and curry leaves and cook, stirring occasionally, for 5 minutes until the onion has softened. Add the ginger and chiles and cook, stirring occasionally, for 1 minute.

Stir in the curry paste and cook, stirring, for 2 minutes, then add the carrots, snow peas, and cauliflower florets. Cook for 5 minutes, then add the tomatoes, peas, and turmeric, and season to taste with salt and pepper. Cook for 3 minutes, then add ⅔ cup of the broth, and bring to a boil.

Transfer the mixture to the slow cooker. If the vegetables are not covered, add more hot broth, then cover, and cook on low for 5 hours until tender. Remove and discard the curry leaves before serving.

Chipotle Chicken

serves 4

4–6 dried chipotle chiles

4 garlic cloves, unpeeled

1 small onion, chopped

One 14.5-ounce can chopped tomatoes

1¼ cups chicken or vegetable broth

Four 6-ounce skinless chicken breasts

Salt and freshly ground pepper, to taste

Preheat the oven to 400°F.

Place the chiles in a bowl and pour in just enough hot water to cover. Set aside to soak for 30 minutes.

Meanwhile, place the unpeeled garlic cloves on a cookie sheet and roast in the preheated oven for about 10 minutes until soft. Remove from the oven and let cool.

Drain the chiles, reserving ½ cup of the soaking water. Seed the chiles, if you like, and chop coarsely. Place the chiles and reserved soaking water in a blender or food processor and process to a puree. Peel and mash the garlic in a bowl.

Place the chile puree, garlic, onion, and tomatoes in the slow cooker and stir in the broth. Season the chicken portions with salt and pepper and place them in the slow cooker. Cover and cook on low for about 5 hours until the chicken is tender and cooked through.

Lift the chicken out of the slow cooker with a slotted spoon, cover, and keep warm. Pour the cooking liquid into a pan and bring to a boil on the stove. Boil for 5–10 minutes until reduced. Place the chicken on warmed plates, spoon the sauce over it, and serve.

Pork with Bell Peppers & Apricots

2 tablespoons olive oil

4 pork chops, trimmed of excess fat

1 shallot, chopped

2 garlic cloves, finely chopped

2 orange bell peppers, seeded and sliced

1 tablespoon all-purpose flour

2½ cups chicken stock

1 tablespoon medium–hot Indian curry paste

½ cup plumped dried apricots

Salt and pepper

Baby spinach leaves and cooked couscous, to serve

Heat the oil in a large skillet. Add the chops and cook over medium heat for 2–4 minutes on each side, until evenly browned. Remove with tongs and put them into the slow cooker.

Add the shallot, garlic, and bell peppers to the skillet, reduce the heat, and cook, stirring occasionally, for 5 minutes, until softened. Stir in the flour and cook, stirring constantly, for 1 minute. Gradually stir in the stock, a little at a time, then add the curry paste and apricots. Bring to a boil, stirring occasionally.

Season to taste with salt and pepper and transfer the mixture to the slow cooker. Cover and cook on low for 8–9 hours, until the meat is tender. Serve immediately with baby spinach and couscous.

Stuffed Cabbage with Tomato Sauce

1 cup finely ground mixed nuts

2 onions, finely chopped

1 garlic clove, finely chopped

2 celery stalks, finely chopped

1 cup grated cheddar cheese

1 teaspoon finely chopped fresh thyme

2 eggs

1 teaspoon yeast extract

12 large green cabbage leaves

Tomato sauce

2 tablespoons sunflower oil

2 onions, chopped

2 garlic cloves, finely chopped

One and a half 14.5 ounce cans chopped tomatoes

2 tablespoons tomato paste

1½ teaspoon sugar

1 bay leaf

Salt and pepper

First, make the tomato sauce. Heat the oil in a heavy pan. Add the onions and cook over medium heat, stirring occasionally, for 5 minutes, until softened. Stir in the garlic and cook for 1 minute, then add the tomatoes, tomato paste, sugar, and bay leaf. Season to taste with salt and pepper and bring to a boil. Reduce the heat and simmer gently for 20 minutes, until thickened.

Meanwhile, combine the nuts, onions, garlic, celery, cheese, and thyme in a bowl. Lightly beat the eggs with the yeast extract in a pitcher, then stir into the nut mixture. Set aside.

Cut out the thick stalk from the cabbage leaves. Blanch the leaves in a large pan of boiling water for 5 minutes, then drain and refresh under cold water. Pat dry with paper towels.

Place a little of the nut mixture on the stalk end of each cabbage leaf. Fold the sides over, then roll up to make a neat package.

Arrange the cabbage rolls in the slow cooker, seam-side down. Remove and discard the bay leaf from the tomato sauce and pour the sauce over the cabbage rolls. Cover and cook on low for 3–4 hours. Serve the cabbage rolls hot or cold.

Tilapia with Fennel & Orange Juice

serves 4

4 whole tilapia, about 12 ounces each, cleaned

1 orange, halved and thinly sliced

2 garlic cloves, thinly sliced

6 fresh thyme sprigs

1 tablespoon olive oil

1 fennel bulb, thinly sliced

2 cups orange juice

1 bay leaf

1 teaspoon dill seeds

Salt and pepper

Salad greens, to serve

Season the fish inside and outside with salt and pepper. Make 3–4 diagonal slashes on each side. Divide the orange slices among the cavities and add 2–3 garlic slices and a thyme sprig to each. Chop the remaining thyme sprigs and put in the slashes with the remaining garlic slices.

Heat the oil in a large skillet. Add the fennel and cook over medium heat, stirring frequently, for 3–5 minutes, until just softened. Add the orange juice and bay leaf and bring to a boil, then reduce the heat and simmer for 5 minutes.

Transfer the fennel mixture to the slow cooker. Put the fish on top and sprinkle with the dill seeds. Cover and cook on high for 1¼–1½ hours, until the flesh flakes easily.

Carefully transfer the fish to 4 warmed plates. Remove and discard the bay leaf and spoon the fennel and some of the cooking juices over the fish. Serve immediately with salad greens.

Vegetable Stew with Dumplings

serves 4

½ butternut squash cut into chunks

2 onions, sliced

2 potatoes, cut into chunks

2 carrots, coarsely chopped

2 celery ribs, sliced

2 zucchini, sliced

2 tablespoons tomato paste

2½ cups hot vegetable broth

1 bay leaf

1 teaspoon ground coriander

½ teaspoon dried thyme

2 cups corn kernels

Salt and freshly ground pepper, to taste

Dumplings

1¾ cups self-rising flour

Pinch of salt

⅔ cup vegetable shortening

2 tablespoons chopped fresh parsley

½ cup milk

Put the butternut squash, onions, potatoes, carrots, celery, and zucchini into the slow cooker. Stir the tomato paste into the broth and pour it over the vegetables. Add the bay leaf, coriander, and thyme and season with salt and pepper. Cover and cook on low for 6 hours.

To make the dumplings, sift the flour with a pinch of salt into a bowl and stir in the shortening and parsley. Add just enough milk to make a firm but light dough. Knead lightly and shape into 12 small balls.

Stir the corn into the vegetable stew and place the dumplings on top. Cook on high for 30 minutes. Serve immediately.

Duck & Red Wine Stew

serves 4

4 duck portions, about 6 ounces each

1 red onion, chopped

2–3 garlic cloves, chopped

1 large carrot, chopped

2 celery stalks, chopped

2 tablespoons all-purpose flour

1¼ cups red wine

2 tablespoons brandy

¾ cup chicken stock or water

3-inch strips thinly pared orange rind

2 tablespoons red currant jelly

1½ cups sugar snap peas

1–2 teaspoon olive oil

1 cup button mushrooms

Salt and pepper

Chopped fresh flat-leaf parsley, to garnish

Heat a heavy skillet for 1 minute, then add the duck portions, and cook over low heat until the fat runs. Increase the heat to medium and cook, turning once, for 5 minutes, until browned on both sides. Using a slotted spoon, transfer to the slow cooker.

Add the onion, garlic, carrot, and celery to the skillet and cook, stirring occasionally, for 5 minutes, until softened. Sprinkle in the flour and cook, stirring constantly, for 2 minutes, then remove the skillet from the heat. Gradually stir in the wine, brandy, and stock, return the skillet to the heat, and bring to a boil, stirring constantly. Season to taste with salt and pepper and stir in the orange rind and red currant jelly.

Pour the mixture over the duck portions, cover, and cook on low, occasionally skimming off the fat from the stew, for 8 hours.

Cook the sugar snap peas in a pan of boiling water for 3 minutes, then drain. Heat the oil in a separate pan, add the mushrooms, and cook, stirring frequently, for 3 minutes. Add the sugar snap peas and mushrooms to the stew, re-cover, and cook on high for 25–30 minutes, until tender. Garnish with parsley and serve immediately.

Three Bean Chili

Serves 4-6

⅔ cup dried red kidney beans, soaked overnight or for at least 5 hours

⅔ cup dried black beans, soaked overnight or for at least 5 hours

⅔ cup dried pinto beans, soaked overnight or for at least 5 hours

2 tablespoons vegetable oil

1 onion, chopped

1 garlic clove, finely chopped

1 fresh red chile, seeded and chopped

1 yellow bell pepper, seeded and chopped

1 teaspoon ground cumin

1 tablespoon chili powder

4 cups vegetable broth

Salt and freshly ground pepper, to taste

1 tablespoon sugar

Chopped fresh cilantro, to garnish

Drain and rinse the beans, place in a saucepan, cover with fresh cold water, and bring to a boil. Boil rapidly for at least 10 minutes, then remove from the heat, drain and rinse again.

Heat the oil in a large, heavy pan. Add the onion, garlic, chile, and bell pepper and cook over medium heat, stirring occasionally, for 5 minutes. Stir in the cumin and chili powder and cook, stirring, for 1–2 minutes. Add the drained beans and stock and bring to a boil. Boil vigorously for 15 minutes.

Transfer the mixture to the slow cooker, cover, and cook on low for 10 hours until the beans are tender.

Season the mixture to taste with salt and pepper, then ladle about one-third into a bowl. Mash well with a potato masher, then return the mashed beans to the cooker, and stir in the sugar. Serve immediately, sprinkled with chopped fresh cilantro.

Chicken & Mushroom Stew

serves 4

1 tablespoon butter

2 tablespoons olive oil

Four 6-ounce skinless chicken parts, such as breasts, thighs, and drumsticks

2 red onions, sliced

2 garlic cloves, finely chopped

One 14.5-ounce can chopped tomatoes

2 tablespoons chopped fresh Italian parsley

6 fresh basil leaves, torn

1 tablespoon sun-dried tomato paste

⅔ cup red wine

4 cups sliced mushrooms

Salt and freshly ground black pepper, to taste

Heat the butter and oil in a heavy skillet. Add the chicken, in batches if necessary, and cook over medium–high heat, turning frequently, for 10 minutes, until golden brown all over. Using a slotted spoon, transfer the chicken to the slow cooker.

Add the onions and garlic to the skillet and cook over low heat, stirring occasionally, for 10 minutes, until translucent. Add the tomatoes with their juices, stir in the parsley, basil, tomato paste, and wine, and season with salt and pepper. Bring to a boil, then pour the mixture over the chicken.

Cover the slow cooker and cook on low for 6½ hours. Stir in the mushrooms, re-cover, and cook on high for 30 minutes, until the chicken is tender and the vegetables are cooked through. Taste and adjust the seasoning, if necessary, and serve.

Lentil & Vegetable Casserole

serves 4

1 onion

10 cloves

1 cup green lentils

1 bay leaf

6¾ cups boiling vegetable broth

2 leeks, washed, trimmed, and sliced

2 potatoes, peeled and diced

2 carrots, chopped

3 zucchini, sliced

1 celery stalk, sliced

1 red bell pepper, seeded and chopped

1 tablespoon lemon juice

Salt and freshly ground pepper, to taste

Peel the onion, stud it with the cloves, and place it in the slow cooker. Add the lentils and bay leaf, pour in the broth, cover, and cook on high for 1½–2 hours.

Remove the onion with a slotted spoon and re-cover the slow cooker. Remove and discard the cloves and slice the onion. Add the onion, leeks, potatoes, carrots, zucchini, celery, and bell pepper to the lentils, season to taste with salt and pepper, re-cover, and cook on high for 3–4 hours, until all the vegetables are tender.

Remove and discard the bay leaf and stir in the lemon juice. Taste and adjust the seasoning if necessary, then serve.

Pork with Apple & Herbs

serves 6

2 tablespoons all-purpose flour

1 pound 12 ounces boneless pork, cut into 1-inch cubes

5 tablespoons sunflower oil

1 large onion, chopped

2 garlic cloves, finely chopped

2 apples, cored and cut into wedges

1¼ cups cider or apple juice

2½ cups chicken stock

2 bay leaves

2 fresh sage sprigs

1 fresh rosemary sprig

3 tablespoons chopped fresh parsley

Salt and pepper

Mashed potatoes, to serve

Put the flour into a plastic food bag and season well with salt and pepper. Add the pork cubes, in batches, hold the top securely, and shake well to coat. Transfer the meat to a plate.

Heat 3 tablespoons of the oil in a large skillet. Add the pork cubes, in batches if necessary, and cook over medium heat, stirring frequently, for 5–8 minutes, until evenly browned. Transfer to a plate and set aside.

Add the remaining oil to the skillet and heat. Add the onion and garlic and cook over low heat, stirring occasionally, for 10 minutes, until softened and lightly browned. Add the apple wedges and cook, stirring occasionally, for 3–5 minutes, until beginning to color. Gradually stir in the hard cider and stock, scraping up any sediment from the bottom of the skillet, and bring to a boil. Season to taste with salt and pepper, add the bay leaves and the sage and rosemary sprigs, and transfer to the slow cooker. Stir in the pork, cover, and cook on low for 6–7 hours.

Remove and discard the bay leaves and the sage and rosemary sprigs. Transfer the stew to warmed individual plates and sprinkle with the parsley. Serve immediately with mashed potatoes.

Neapolitan Beef

1¼ cups red wine

4 tablespoons olive oil

1 celery stalk, chopped

2 shallots, sliced

4 garlic cloves, finely chopped

1 bay leaf

10 fresh basil leaves, plus extra to garnish

3 fresh parsley sprigs

Pinch of grated nutmeg

Pinch of ground cinnamon

2 cloves

3 pounds 6 ounce beef pot roast

1–2 garlic cloves, thinly sliced

2 slices bacon, chopped

one 14.5-ounce can chopped tomatoes

2 tablespoons tomato paste

Combine the wine, half the oil, the celery, shallots, garlic, herbs, and spices in a large nonmetallic bowl. Add the beef, cover, and let marinate, turning occasionally, for 12 hours.

Drain the beef, reserving the marinade, and pat dry with paper towels. Make small incisions all over the beef using a sharp knife. Insert a slice of garlic and a piece of bacon in each "pocket." Heat the remaining oil in a large skillet. Add the meat and cook over medium heat, turning frequently, until evenly browned. Transfer the beef to the slow cooker.

Strain the reserved marinade into the skillet and bring to a boil. Stir in the tomatoes and tomato paste. Stir well, then pour the mixture over the beef. Cover and cook on low for about 8–9 hours, until the beef is cooked to your liking. If possible, turn the beef over halfway through the cooking time and re-cover the slow cooker immediately.

Remove the beef from the slow cooker and place on a carving board. Cover with foil and let stand for 10–15 minutes to firm up. Cut into slices and transfer to a platter. Spoon the sauce over it, garnish with basil leaves, and serve immediately.

Spicy Chicken with Sausage and Peppers

serves 4

1½ tablespoons all-purpose flour

Salt and freshly ground pepper, to taste

Four 6-ounce skinless chicken parts, such as breasts, thighs, and drumsticks

2 tablespoons olive oil

1 onion, chopped

2–3 garlic cloves, chopped

1 fresh red chile, seeded and chopped

8 ounces chorizo or other spicy sausages, skinned and cut into small chunks

1¼ cups chicken broth

⅔ cup dry white wine

1 tablespoon dark soy sauce

1 large red bell pepper, seeded and sliced into rings

1⅔ cups fava beans

¼ cup arugula or baby spinach leaves

Spread out the flour on a plate and season well with salt and pepper. Toss the chicken in the seasoned flour until thoroughly coated, shaking off any excess. Reserve any remaining flour.

Heat 1 tablespoon oil in a heavy skillet, add the chicken parts, and cook over medium–high heat, turning frequently, for 10 minutes, or until golden brown all over. Add a little more oil during cooking if necessary. Using a slotted spoon, transfer the chicken to the slow cooker.

Add the remaining oil to the skillet. Add the onion, garlic, and chile and cook over low heat, stirring occasionally, for 5 minutes, until softened. Add the chorizo and cook, stirring frequently, for an additional 2 minutes. Sprinkle in the remaining flour and cook, stirring constantly, for 2 minutes, then remove the skillet from the heat. Gradually stir in the broth, wine, and soy sauce, then return the skillet to the heat, and bring to a boil, stirring constantly. Pour the onion mixture over the chicken, then cover and cook on low for 6½ hours.

Add the red bell pepper and beans to the slow cooker, re-cover, and cook on high for 45–60 minutes, until the chicken and vegetables are cooked through and tender. Season to taste with salt and pepper, stir in the arugula, and let stand for 2 minutes, until just wilted, then serve.

Jalapeño Pork Chops

**4 pork chops, trimmed
of excess fat**

2 tablespoons corn oil

**One 15-ounce can
pineapple chunks in
juice**

**1 red bell pepper,
seeded and finely
chopped**

**2 fresh jalapeño chiles,
seeded and finely
chopped**

1 onion, finely chopped

**1 tablespoon chopped
fresh cilantro, plus
extra sprigs to garnish**

½ cup hot chicken stock

Salt and pepper

Flour tortillas, to serve

Season the chops with salt and pepper to taste. Heat the oil
in a large heavy skillet. Add the chops and cook over
medium heat for 2–3 minutes each side, until lightly
browned. Transfer them to the slow cooker. Drain the
pineapple, reserving the juice, and set aside.

Add the bell pepper, chiles, and onion to the skillet and
cook, stirring occasionally, for 5 minutes, until the onion
has softened. Transfer the mixture to the slow cooker and
add the chopped cilantro, stock, and ½ cup of the reserved
pineapple juice. Cover and cook on low for 6 hours, until
the chops are tender.

Add the reserved pineapple to the slow cooker, re-cover,
and cook on high for 15 minutes. Garnish with cilantro
sprigs and serve immediately with flour tortillas.

Chicken with New Potatoes & Bacon

serves 6

1 chicken, weighing 4 pounds

4 tablespoons butter

2 tablespoons olive oil

1 pound 7 ounces small white onions, peeled

1 pound 7 ounces small new potatoes

6 slices bacon, chopped

2¼ cups dry white wine

1 bay leaf

1 tablespoon dried mixed herbs

2¼ cups hot chicken stock

Salt and pepper chopped fresh flat-leaf parsley, to garnish

Season the chicken inside and out with salt and pepper. Melt half the butter with the oil in a large skillet. Add the chicken and cook over medium heat, turning frequently, for 8–10 minutes, until evenly browned. Remove from the pan and put it into the slow cooker, breast-side down.

Add the onions, potatoes, and bacon to the skillet and cook, stirring frequently, for 10 minutes, until lightly browned. Pour in the wine, season to taste with salt and pepper, and add the bay leaf and mixed herbs. Bring to a boil, then transfer the mixture to the slow cooker. Pour in the hot stock. Cover and cook, turning the chicken once halfway through cooking, for 5–6 hours, until the chicken is tender and cooked through.

Using a slotted spoon, transfer the vegetables and bacon to a bowl. Carefully remove the chicken and put it on a warmed serving dish. Arrange the vegetables around the chicken and keep warm. Remove and discard the bay leaf.

Measure 2½ cups of the cooking liquid, pour it into a pan, and bring to a boil. Boil until slightly reduced, then whisk in the remaining butter, a little at a time. Pour the sauce into a sauceboat. Carve the chicken and transfer to individual plates with the bacon and vegetables. Garnish with parsley and serve immediately with the sauce.

Cured Ham Cooked in Cider

serves 6

2 pounds 4 ounces boneless cured ham in a single piece

1 onion, halved

4 cloves

6 black peppercorns

1 teaspoon juniper berries (optional)

1 celery stalk, chopped

1 carrot, sliced

3 cups cider

Fresh vegetables, such as mashed potatoes and peas, to serve

Place a trivet or rack in the slow cooker, if you like, and stand the ham on it. Otherwise, just place the ham in the cooker. Stud each of the onion halves with 2 cloves and add to the cooker with the peppercorns, juniper berries, celery, and carrot.

Pour in the hard cider, cover, and cook on low for 8 hours until the meat is tender.

Remove the ham from the cooker and place on a board. Tent with foil and let stand for 10–15 minutes. Discard the cooking liquid and flavorings.

Cut off any rind and fat from the ham, then carve into slices, and serve with fresh vegetables.

Slow Cooker Salmon

serves 4

⅔ cup fish stock

1 cup dry white wine

2 lemons

1 onion, thinly sliced

4 salmon fillets, about 6 ounces each

1 tablespoon dried mixed herbs

3 pounds spinach, coarse stalks removed

freshly grated nutmeg, to taste

¾ cup (1½ sticks) unsalted butter, plus extra for greasing

Salt and pepper

Lightly grease a slow cooker pot with butter. Pour the stock and wine into a pan and bring to a boil. Meanwhile, thinly slice 1 of the lemons. Put half the lemon slices and all the onion slices over the bottom of the slow cooker pot and top with the salmon fillets. Season to taste with salt and pepper, add the mixed herbs, and cover the fish with the remaining lemon slices. Pour the hot stock mixture over the fish, cover, and cook on low for 1½ hours, until the fish flakes easily.

Meanwhile, grate the rind and squeeze the juice from the remaining lemon. When the fish is nearly ready, cook the spinach, in just the water clinging to the leaves after washing, for 3–5 minutes, until wilted. Drain well, squeezing out as much water as possible. Chop finely, arrange on warmed individual plates, and season to taste with salt, pepper, and nutmeg.

Carefully lift the fish out of the slow cooker and discard the lemon slices, onion slices. Put the salmon fillets on top of the spinach and keep warm.

Melt the butter in a pan over low heat. Stir in the lemon rind and half the juice. Taste and adjust the seasoning, adding more lemon juice, salt, and pepper if needed. Pour the lemon butter sauce over the fish and serve immediately.

Nutty chicken

3 tablespoons sunflower oil

4 skinless chicken portions

2 shallots, chopped

1 teaspoon ground ginger

1 tablespoon all-purpose flour

2 cups beef stock

½ cup walnut pieces

Grated rind of 1 lemon

2 tablespoons lemon juice

1 tablespoon molasses

Salt and pepper

Fresh watercress or mizuna sprigs, to garnish

Heat the oil in a large, heavy skillet. Season the chicken portions with salt and pepper and add to the skillet. Cook over medium heat, turning occasionally, for 5–8 minutes, until lightly golden all over. Transfer to the slow cooker.

Add the shallots to the skillet and cook, stirring occasionally, for 3–4 minutes until softened. Sprinkle in the ginger and flour and cook, stirring constantly, for 1 minute. Gradually stir in the stock and bring to a boil, stirring constantly. Lower the heat and simmer for 1 minute, then stir in the nuts, lemon rind and juice, and molasses.

Pour the sauce over the chicken. Cover and cook on low for 6 hours until the chicken is cooked through and tender. Taste and adjust the seasoning if necessary. Transfer the chicken to warm bowls, spoon some of the sauce over each portion, garnish with watercress sprigs, and serve immediately.

Rich Beef & Coffee Stew

serves 6

4 tablespoons sunflower oil

3 pounds braising beef, cut into 1-inch cubes

4 onions, sliced

1 garlic clove, finely chopped

5 tablespoons all-purpose flour

1¼ cups red wine

pinch of dried oregano

1 small fresh rosemary sprig

2¼ cups black coffee

Salt and pepper

Fresh marjoram sprigs, to garnish

Mashed sweet potatoes, to serve

Heat the oil in a large skillet. Add the beef and cook over medium heat, stirring frequently, for 8–10 minutes, until evenly browned. Transfer to the slow cooker with a slotted spoon.

Add the onions and garlic to the skillet, reduce the heat, and cook, stirring occasionally, for 10 minutes, until softened and just beginning to color. Stir in the flour and cook, stirring constantly, for 1 minute. Gradually stir in the wine, a little at a time. Add the oregano and rosemary sprig and season to taste with salt and pepper. Pour in the coffee and bring to a boil, stirring constantly.

Transfer the mixture to the slow cooker. Cover and cook on low for 8–9 hours, until the meat is tender. Remove and discard the rosemary sprig. Taste and adjust the seasoning, adding salt and pepper if needed. Garnish with marjoram sprigs and serve immediately with mashed sweet potatoes.

Chicken with Red Bell Pepper & Fava Beans

1½ tablespoons all-purpose flour

4 chicken portions, about 6 ounces each

2 tablespoons olive oil

1 onion, chopped

2–3 garlic cloves, chopped

1 fresh red chile, seeded and chopped

8 ounces chorizo or other spicy sausages, skinned and cut into small chunks

1¼ cups chicken stock

⅔ cup dry white wine

1 tablespoon dark soy sauce

1 large red bell pepper, seeded and sliced into rings

1⅔ cups shelled fava beans

¼ cup arugula or baby spinach leaves

Salt and pepper

Spread out the flour on a plate and season well with salt and pepper. Toss the chicken in the flour until thoroughly coated, shaking off any excess. Reserve any remaining flour.

Heat half the oil in a heavy skillet, add the chicken portions, and cook over medium–high heat, turning frequently, for 10 minutes, or until golden brown all over. Add a little more oil during cooking if necessary. Using a slotted spoon, transfer the chicken to the slow cooker.

Add the remaining oil to the skillet. Add the onion, garlic, and chile and cook over low heat, stirring occasionally, for 5 minutes, until softened. Add the chorizo and cook, stirring frequently, for a further 2 minutes. Sprinkle in the remaining flour and cook, stirring constantly, for 2 minutes, then remove the skillet from the heat. Gradually stir in the stock, wine, and soy sauce, then return the skillet to the heat, and bring to a boil, stirring constantly. Pour the onion mixture over the chicken, then cover and cook on low for 6½ hours.

Add the red bell pepper and beans to the slow cooker, re-cover, and cook on high for 45–60 minutes, until the chicken and vegetables are cooked through and tender. Season to taste with salt and pepper, stir in the arugula, and let stand for 2 minutes, until just wilted, then serve.

Louisiana Zucchini

serves 6

2 pound 4 ounces zucchini, thickly sliced

1 onion, finely chopped

2 garlic cloves, finely chopped

2 red bell peppers, seeded and chopped

5 tablespoons hot vegetable stock

4 tomatoes, peeled and chopped

2 tablespoons butter, diced

Salt and cayenne pepper

Place the zucchini, onion, garlic, and bell peppers in the slow cooker and season to taste with salt and cayenne pepper.

Pour in the stock and mix well.

Sprinkle the chopped tomatoes on top and dot with the butter. Cover and cook on high for 2½ hours until tender.

Beef Stew with Olives

serves 4-6

2 pounds braising beef, cubed

2 onions, thinly sliced

2 carrots, sliced

4 large garlic cloves, lightly crushed

1 bouquet garni

4 juniper berries

2¼ cups dry red wine

2 tablespoons brandy

2 tablespoons olive oil

3 tablespoons all-purpose flour

⅔ cup diced bacon

2 x 4-inch strips of thinly pared orange rind

¾ cup pitted black olives, rinsed

Salt and pepper

Buttered noodles or tagliatelle, to serve

To garnish
1 tablespoon chopped fresh flat-leaf parsley
finely grated orange rind

Put the stewing steak in a large, nonmetallic dish, add the onions, carrots, garlic, bouquet garni, and juniper berries, and season with salt and pepper. Combine the wine, brandy, and olive oil in a pitcher and pour the mixture over the meat and vegetables. Cover with plastic wrap and marinate in the refrigerator for 24 hours.

Using a slotted spoon remove the steak from the marinade and pat dry with paper towels. Reserve the marinade, vegetables, and flavorings. Place the flour in a shallow dish and season well with salt and pepper. Toss the steak cubes in the flour until well coated and shake off any excess.

Sprinkle half the bacon in the base of the slow cooker and top with the steak cubes. Pour in the marinade, including the vegetables and flavorings, and add the strips of orange rind and the olives. Top with the remaining bacon. Cover and cook on low for 9½–10 hours, until the steak and vegetables are tender.

Remove and discard the bouquet garni and skim off any fat that has risen to the surface of the stew. Sprinkle the parsley and grated rind over the top and serve with buttered noodles or tagliatelle.

Lamb Stew with Red Bell Peppers

serves 4

1½ tablespoons all-purpose flour

1 teaspoons ground cloves

1 pound boneless lamb, cut into thin strips

1–1½ tablespoons olive oil

1 white onion, sliced

2–3 garlic cloves, sliced

1¼ cups orange juice

⅔ cup lamb or chicken stock

1 cinnamon stick

2 red bell peppers, seeded and sliced into rings

4 tomatoes, coarsely chopped

4 fresh cilantro sprigs

Salt and freshly ground pepper, to taste

1 tablespoon chopped fresh cilantro, to garnish

Combine the flour and ground cloves in a shallow dish, add the strips of lamb, and toss well to coat, shaking off any excess. Reserve the remaining spiced flour.

Heat 1 tablespoon of the oil in a heavy skillet, add the lamb, and cook over high heat, stirring frequently, for 3 minutes, until browned all over. Using a slotted spoon, transfer the lamb to the slow cooker.

Add the onion and garlic to the skillet, with the remaining oil if necessary, and cook over low heat, stirring occasionally, for 5 minutes, until softened. Sprinkle in the reserved spiced flour and cook, stirring constantly, for 2 minutes, then remove the skillet from the heat. Gradually stir in the orange juice and stock, then return the skillet to the heat, and bring to a boil, stirring constantly.

Pour the mixture over the lamb, add the cinnamon stick, bell peppers, tomatoes, and cilantro sprigs, and stir well. Cover and cook on low for 7–8 hours, until the meat is tender.

Remove and discard the cinnamon stick and cilantro sprigs. Season to taste with salt and pepper, sprinkle the stew with chopped cilantro. Ideal served with mashed sweet potatoes with scallions and green vegetables.

Chicken Stew

3 tablespoons corn oil

1 large onion, thinly sliced

1 green bell pepper, seeded and chopped

8 chicken pieces, such as thighs and drumsticks

One 14.5 ounces can chopped tomatoes, drained

Pinch of cayenne pepper

1 tablespoon Worcestershire sauce

1¼ cups boiling chicken stock

1 tablespoon cornstarch

1 cup frozen corn, thawed

3 cups frozen fava beans, thawed

Salt

Crusty bread, to serve

Heat the oil in a large, heavy skillet. Add the onion and bell pepper and cook over medium heat, stirring occasionally, for 5 minutes until the onion is softened. Using a slotted spoon, transfer the mixture to the slow cooker.

Add the chicken to the skillet and cook, turning occasionally, for 5 minutes until golden all over. Transfer to the slow cooker and add the tomatoes. Season with a pinch of cayenne pepper and salt. Stir the Worcestershire sauce into the hot stock and pour into the slow cooker. Cover and cook on low for 6½ hours.

Mix the cornstarch to a paste with 2–3 tablespoons water and stir into the stew. Add the corn and beans, re-cover, and cook on high for 30–40 minutes until everything is cooked through and piping hot. Transfer to warm plates and serve with crusty bread.

Thick Beef & Pearl Onion Casserole

Serves 6

2 tablespoons olive oil

1 pound pearl onions, peeled but left whole

2 garlic cloves, halved

2 pounds chuck or other braising beef, cubed

½ teaspoon ground cinnamon

1 teaspoon ground cloves

1 teaspoon ground cumin

2 tablespoons tomato paste

3 cups red wine

Grated rind and juice of 1 orange

1 bay leaf

Salt and freshly ground pepper, to taste

1 tablespoon chopped fresh Italian parsley, to garnish

Boiled potatoes, to serve

Heat the oil in a heavy skillet. Add the onions and garlic and cook over medium heat, stirring frequently, for 5 minutes, until softened and beginning to brown. Increase the heat to high, add the beef, and cook, stirring frequently, for 5 minutes, until browned all over.

Stir in the cinnamon, cloves, cumin, and tomato paste, and season with salt and pepper. Pour in the wine, scraping up any sediment from the base of the skillet. Stir in the orange rind and juice, add the bay leaf, and bring to a boil.

Transfer the mixture to the slow cooker, cover and cook on low for 9 hours, until the beef is tender. If possible, stir the stew once during the second half of the cooking time.

Serve the stew garnished with the parsley and accompanied by boiled potatoes.

Chicken Braised with Red Cabbage

Serves 4

2 tablespoons vegetable oil

Four 6-ounce skinless chicken thighs or drumsticks

1 onion, chopped

5½ cups shredded red cabbage

2 apples, peeled, cored, and chopped

12 canned or cooked chestnuts, halved (optional)

½ cup red wine

6 juniper berries (optional)

Salt and freshly ground black pepper, to taste

Fresh parsley, to garnish

Heat the oil in a large, heavy pan. Add the chicken and cook, turning frequently, for 5 minutes until golden on all sides. Using a slotted spoon transfer to a plate lined with paper towels.

Add the onion to the pan and cook over medium heat, stirring occasionally, until softened. Stir in the cabbage and the apples and cook, stirring occasionally, for 5 minutes. Add the chestnuts, if using, juniper berries, and wine and season to taste with salt and pepper. Bring to a boil.

Spoon half the cabbage mixture into the slow cooker, add the chicken pieces, then top with the remaining cabbage mixture. Cover and cook on low for 5 hours until the chicken is tender and cooked through. Serve immediately, garnished with the fresh parsley.

Vegetarian Paella

serves 6

4 tablespoons olive oil

1 yellow onion, sliced

2 garlic cloves, finely chopped

4 cups hot vegetable stock

large pinch of saffron threads, lightly crushed

1 yellow bell pepper, seeded and sliced

1 red bell pepper, seeded and sliced

1 large eggplant, diced

1½ cups paella or risotto rice

6 medium tomatoes peeled and chopped

1½ cups sliced cremini mushrooms

1 cup halved green beans

One 15-ounce can borlotti beans, drained and rinsed

Salt and pepper

Heat the oil in a large skillet. Add the onion and garlic and cook over low heat, stirring occasionally, for 5 minutes, until softened. Meanwhile, put 3 tablespoons of the hot stock into a small bowl and stir in the saffron, then let steep.

Add the bell peppers and eggplant to the skillet and cook, stirring occasionally, for 5 minutes. Add the rice and cook, stirring constantly, for 1 minute, until the grains are coated with oil and glistening. Pour in the remaining stock and add the tomatoes, mushrooms, green beans, and borlotti beans. Stir in the saffron mixture and season to taste with salt and pepper.

Transfer the mixture to the slow cooker, cover, and cook on low for 2½–3 hours, until the rice is tender and stock has been absorbed. Serve immediately.

Fettuccini with Shrimp & Tomato Sauce

serves 4

One 14.5-ounce can chopped tomatoes

6 tablespoons tomato paste

1 garlic clove, finely chopped

2 tablespoons chopped fresh parsley

Salt and freshly ground pepper, to taste

1 pound 2 ounces cooked, peeled large shrimp

6 fresh basil leaves, torn

1 pound dried fettuccini

Fresh basil leaves, to garnish

Put the tomatoes, tomato paste, garlic, and parsley in the slow cooker and season to taste with salt and pepper. Cover and cook on low for 7 hours.

Add the shrimp and basil. Re-cover and cook on high for 15 minutes.

Meanwhile, bring a large pan of lightly salted water to a boil. Add the pasta, bring back to a boil, and cook for 10–12 minutes until tender but still firm to the bite.

Drain the pasta and tip it into a warm serving bowl. Add the shrimp sauce and toss lightly. Garnish with the basil leaves and serve immediately.

Chinese Beef

serves 6

4 dried Chinese tree ear mushrooms

4 tablespoons peanut oil

2 pound 4 ounces top round steak, cut into 1-inch cubes

3 tablespoons dark soy sauce

2 tablespoons Chinese rice wine or dry sherry

1 tablespoon tomato paste

1-inch piece fresh ginger, very finely chopped

2 garlic cloves, very finely chopped

2 tablespoons light brown sugar

1 teaspoon Chinese five-spice powder

3 cups beef stock

5 carrots, thinly sliced diagonally

Cooked egg noodles, to serve

Put the mushrooms into a heatproof bowl and pour in warm water to cover. Set aside to soak for 20 minutes.

Meanwhile, heat the oil in a large pan. Add the beef, in batches, and cook over medium heat, stirring frequently, for 8–10 minutes, until evenly browned. Remove with a slotted spoon and drain on paper towels.

Drain the mushrooms, discarding the soaking water, and gently squeeze out any excess liquid. Cut off and discard the stems, slice the caps, and put them into a bowl. Add the soy sauce, rice wine, tomato paste, ginger, garlic, sugar, five-spice powder, and stock and mix well.

When all the meat has been browned, wipe out the pan with paper towels. Return the meat to the pan, stir in the mushroom mixture, and bring to a boil.

Transfer the mixture to the slow cooker, cover, and cook on low for 8 hours, until the meat is tender. Stir in the carrots, re-cover, and cook on high for an additional 45–60 minutes, until the carrots are tender. Serve immediately with noodles.

Pork & Vegetable Ragout

1 pound lean, boneless pork

1½ tablespoons all-purpose flour

1 teaspoon ground coriander

1 teaspoon ground cumin

1½ teaspoons ground cinnamon

1 tablespoon olive oil

1 onion, chopped

One 14.5-ounce can chopped tomatoes

2 tablespoons tomato paste

1¼ cups chicken broth

2-3 carrots, chopped

2 pounds winter squash (such as kabocha or acorn), peeled and chopped

1 pound leeks, trimmed, blanched, drained, and sliced

½ cup okra, trimmed and sliced

Salt and freshly ground pepper, to taste

Fresh parsley sprigs, to garnish

Couscous, to serve

Trim off any visible fat from the pork and cut the flesh into thin strips about 2 inches long. Combine the flour, coriander, cumin, and cinnamon in a shallow dish, add the pork strips, and toss well to coat. Shake off the excess and reserve the remaining spiced flour.

Heat the oil in a heavy skillet. Add the onion and cook over low heat, stirring occasionally, for 5 minutes, until softened. Add the pork strips, increase the heat to high, and cook, stirring frequently, for 5 minutes, until browned all over. Sprinkle in the reserved spiced flour and cook, stirring constantly, for 2 minutes, then remove the skillet from the heat.

Gradually stir in the tomatoes with their can juices. Combine the tomato paste with the broth in a pitcher, then gradually stir the mixture into the skillet. Add the carrots, return the skillet to the heat, and bring to a boil, stirring constantly.

Transfer to the slow cooker, stir in the squash, leeks, and okra, and season to taste with salt and pepper. Cover and cook on low for 5–6 hours, until the meat and vegetables are tender. Garnish with parsley sprigs and serve with couscous.

Spring Vegetable Stew

serves 4

2 tablespoons olive oil

4–8 pearl onions, halved

2 celery ribs, cut into ¼-inch slices

12 baby carrots, halved if large

⅔ pound (4-6) new potatoes, halved

4–5 cups vegetable broth

1¼ cups dried cannellini beans, soaked overnight or for at least 5 hours

1 bouquet garni

2 tablespoons light soy sauce

¾ cup baby corn

⅔ cup shelled fava beans, thawed if frozen

2½ cups shredded Savoy cabbage

1½ tablespoons cornstarch

Salt and freshly ground pepper, to taste

1 cup freshly grated Parmesan cheese, to serve

Drain and rinse the beans, place in a saucepan, cover with fresh cold water, and bring to a boil. Boil rapidly for at least 10 minutes, then remove from the heat, drain and rinse again.

Heat the oil in a pan. Add the onions, celery, carrots, and potatoes and cook over low heat, stirring frequently, for 5–8 minutes, until softened. Add the broth, cannelloni beans, bouquet garni, and soy sauce, bring to a boil, then transfer to the slow cooker.

Add the corn, fava beans, and cabbage, season to taste with salt and pepper, and stir well. Cover and cook on high for 3–4 hours, until the vegetables are tender.

Remove and discard the bouquet garni. Stir the cornstarch with 3 tablespoons water to a paste in a small bowl, then stir into the stew. Re-cover and cook on high for a further 15 minutes, until thickened. Serve the stew with the Parmesan cheese on the side.

Lamb Shanks with Olives

1½ tablespoons all-purpose fl our

4 lamb shanks

2 tablespoons olive oil

1 onion, sliced

2 garlic cloves, fi nely chopped

2 teaspoons sweet paprika

One 14.5-ounce can chopped tomatoes

2 tablespoons tomato paste

2 carrots, sliced

2 teaspoons sugar

1 cup red wine

2-cinnamon stick

2 fresh rosemary sprigs

1 cup pitted black olives

2 tablespoons lemon juice

2 tablespoons chopped fresh mint, plus extra leaves to garnish

Salt and pepper

Put the flour into a plastic food bag and season to taste with salt and pepper. Add the lamb shanks, hold the top securely, and shake well to coat.

Heat the oil in a large heavy pan. Add the lamb shanks and cook over medium heat, turning frequently, for 6–8 minutes, until evenly browned. Transfer to a plate and set aside.

Add the onion and garlic to the pan and cook, stirring frequently, for 5 minutes, until softened. Stir in the paprika and cook for 1 minute. Add the tomatoes, tomato paste, carrots, sugar, wine, cinnamon stick, and rosemary sprigs and bring to a boil.

Transfer the mixture to the slow cooker and add the lamb shanks. Cover and cook on low for 8 hours, until the lamb is very tender.

Add the olives, lemon juice, and chopped mint to the slow cooker. Re-cover and cook on high for 30 minutes. Remove and discard the rosemary sprigs and cinnamon stick. Garnish with mint leaves and serve immediately.

Chile Chicken

2 tablespoons sunflower oil

6 chicken portions

2 onions, chopped

2 garlic cloves, chopped

1 fresh chile, seeded and chopped

6 tomatoes, peeled and chopped

2 teaspoons sweet paprika

1 bay leaf

1 cup hot chicken stock

Salt and pepper

Heat the oil in a heavy skillet. Add the chicken and cook over a medium heat, turning occasionally for about 10 minutes until browned.

Transfer the chicken to the slow cooker and add the onions, garlic, chile and tomatoes. Sprinkle in the paprika, add the bay leaf, and pour in the stock. Season to taste with salt and pepper.

Stir well, cover and cook on low for 6 hours, until the chicken is cooked and tender. Remove and discard the bay leaf. Serve immediately.

Pork with Almonds

2 tablespoons sunflower oil

2 onions, chopped

2 garlic cloves, finely chopped

2-inch cinnamon stick

3 cloves

1 cup ground almonds

1 pound 10 ounce boneless pork, cut into 1-inch cubes

4 tomatoes, peeled and chopped

2 tablespoons capers

1 cup green olives, pitted

3 pickled jalapeño chiles, drained, seeded, and cut into rings

1½ cups chicken stock

Salt and pepper

Fresh cilantro sprigs, to garnish (optional)

Heat half the oil in a large, heavy skillet. Add the onions and cook over low heat, stirring occasionally, for 5 minutes until softened. Add the garlic, cinnamon, cloves, and almonds and cook, stirring frequently, for 8–10 minutes. Be careful not to burn the almonds.

Remove and discard the spices and transfer the mixture to a food processor. Process to a smooth purée.

Rinse out the skillet and return to the heat. Heat the remaining oil, then add the pork, in batches if necessary. Cook over medium heat, stirring frequently, for 5–10 minutes until browned all over. Return all the pork to the skillet and add the almond purée, tomatoes, capers, olives, chiles, and chicken stock. Bring to a boil, then transfer to the slow cooker.

Season with salt and pepper and mix well. Cover and cook on low for 5 hours. To serve, transfer to warmed plates and garnish with cilantro sprigs, if desired.

3

Salads and Side Dishes

Roast Summer Vegetables

serves 4

2 tablespoons olive oil

1 fennel bulb, cut into wedges

2 red onions, cut into wedges

2 beefsteak tomatoes, cut into wedges

1 eggplant, thickly sliced

2 zucchini, thickly sliced

1 yellow bell pepper, seeded and cut into chunks

1 red bell pepper, seeded and cut into chunks

1 orange bell pepper, seeded and cut into chunks

4 garlic cloves

4 fresh rosemary sprigs

pepper

Crusty bread, to serve (optional)

Brush an ovenproof dish with a little oil. Arrange the fennel, onions, tomatoes, eggplant, zucchini, and bell peppers in the dish and tuck the garlic cloves and rosemary sprigs among them. Drizzle with the remaining oil and season to taste with pepper.

Roast the vegetables in a preheated oven, 400°F for 10 minutes. Turn the vegetables over, return the dish to the oven, and roast for an additional 10–15 minutes or until the vegetables are tender and beginning to turn golden brown.

Serve the vegetables straight from the dish or transfer to a warm serving platter. Serve immediately, with crusty bread, if using, to soak up the juices.

Mozzarella Cheese & Tomato Salad

serves 4

1 pound cherry tomatoes

4 scallions

½ cup extra virgin olive oil

2 tablespoons best-quality balsamic vinegar

1½ cups buffalo mozzarella cheese, cut into cubes

½ cup fresh flat-leaf parsley

1 cup fresh basil leaves

Salt and pepper

Using a sharp knife, cut the tomatoes in half and put in a large bowl. Trim the scallions, finely chop the green and white parts, then add to the bowl.

Pour in the oil and vinegar and use your hands to toss together. Season with salt and pepper, add the mozzarella cheese and toss again. Cover and chill for 4 hours.

Remove the salad from the refrigerator 10 minutes before serving. Finely chop the parsley and add to the salad. Tear the basil leaves over the salad and toss all the ingredients together again. Adjust the seasoning and serve.

Zucchini Fritters

makes 16-30

⅓ cup self–rising flour

2 eggs, beaten

¼ cup milk

2 zucchini

2 tablespoons fresh thyme

1 tablespoon oil

Salt and pepper

Sift the flour into a large bowl and make a well in the center. Add the eggs to the well and, using a wooden spoon, gradually draw in the flour.

Slowly add the milk to the mixture, stirring continuously to form a thick batter.

Meanwhile, wash the zucchini. Grate them over a paper towel placed in a bowl to absorb some of the juices.

Add the zucchini, thyme, and salt and pepper to taste to the batter and mix thoroughly.

Heat the oil in a large heavy-bottom skillet. Taking a tablespoon of the batter for a medium-size fritter or half a tablespoon of batter for a smaller fritter, spoon the mixture into the hot oil and cook, in batches, for 3–4 minutes on each side.

Remove the fritters with a slotted spoon and drain thoroughly on absorbent paper towels. Keep each batch of fritters warm in the oven while making the rest. Transfer to warmed serving plates and serve hot.

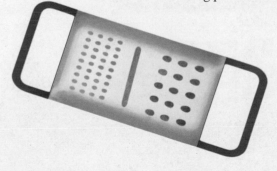

Boston Baked Beans

serves 10

1 pound dry navy beans

6 cups water

Pinch of baking soda

1 bay leaf

6 strips bacon, cut in ½-inch pieces (traditionally salt pork is used, and if desired 4 ounces can be substituted for the bacon)

1 yellow onion, diced

⅓ cup molasses

¼ cup packed dark brown sugar

1 teaspoon dry mustard

1½ teaspoon salt, or to taste

½ teaspoon freshly ground black pepper

Pre-heat oven to 300°F.

Soak the beans in the 6 cups of water overnight in a large saucepan or Dutch oven. Add a pinch of baking soda and bay leaf, and bring to a boil. Reduce the heat to medium and simmer for 10 minutes. Drain into a colander set over a large bowl, and reserve the liquid.

Transfer the drained beans into a small Dutch oven, or a 2 ½-quart bean pot if you have one, and add the rest of the ingredients. Stir until combined. Add enough of the reserved water to just barely cover the beans.

Cover the pot tightly and place in the oven for 1 hour. Uncover and check the liquid level. Add some more reserved liquid if the beans are getting too dry. Cover and cook 1 more hour. Uncover and test the beans; they should be starting to get tender, but if they're still firm, cover and cook a bit longer, adding a splash of water if they're getting too dry.

When just tender, turn the heat up to 350 degrees F., and continue to cook uncovered for another 30 minutes or so. This last 30 minutes is to reduce the liquid a bit, to create a thick, syrupy consistency. Remove when ready, and serve hot or room temperature.

Note: The cooking times will vary based on the size and shape of the baking vessel, but the process will not. Simply bake the beans covered until just tender, and finish uncovered until the liquid has thickened slightly.

Steakhouse Creamed Spinach

serves 4-6

½ cup (1 stick) unsalted butter

24 ounces pre-washed, ready-to-use baby spinach

½ onion, finely diced

1 whole clove

3 cloves garlic, very finely minced

⅓ cup flour

1½ cups cold milk

Pinch freshly ground nutmeg

Salt and pepper, to taste

Put a large stockpot over high heat. Add 1 tablespoon of the butter, and as soon as it melts, dump in all the spinach and cover quickly. Leave for one minute, uncover, and continue cooking, stirring the spinach with a long wooden spoon, until just barely wilted. Transfer to a colander to drain.

When the spinach is cool enough to handle, squeeze as much liquid out as possible, and roughly chop. Press between paper towels to draw out the last of the water, and reserve until needed.

Melt the rest of the butter in a saucepan over medium heat. Add the onions and cook for about 5 minutes, or until translucent. Whisk in the flour and cook for 3 minutes, stirring. Add the garlic and cook for 1 minute. Pour in the cold milk, whisking constantly, and cook until it comes to a simmer. Reduce heat to low and simmer for another 5 minutes. The sauce will thicken as it cooks.

Season the sauce with nutmeg, salt and fresh ground black pepper to taste. Add the spinach, and stir to combine. The dish is ready to serve as soon as the spinach is heated through. Taste once more, and adjust seasoning before serving.

Perfect Mashed Potatoes

serves 4

2 pounds of potatoes, such as Russet potatoes

½ stick butter

3 tablespoons milk

Salt and pepper

Peel the potatoes, placing them in cold water as you prepare the others to prevent them from going brown.

Cut the potatoes into even-sized chunks and cook in a large saucepan of boiling salted water over a medium heat, covered, for 20 to 25 minutes until they are tender. Test with the point of a knife, but do make sure you test right to the middle to avoid lumps.

Remove the pan from the heat and drain the potatoes. Return the potatoes to the hot pan and mash with a potato masher until smooth.

Add the butter and continue to mash until it is all mixed in, then add the milk.

Taste the mash and season with salt and pepper as necessary. Serve at once.

Variations: For herb mash, mix in 3 tablespoons chopped fresh parsley, thyme or mint. For mustard or horseradish mash, mix in 2 tablespoons wholegrain mustard or horseradish sauce. For pesto mash, stir in 4 tablespoons fresh pesto and for nutmeg mash, grate ½ a nutmeg into the mash and add 4 fl ounces natural yogurt. To make creamed potato, add 4 fl ounces soured cream and 2 tablespoons snipped fresh chives.

Deli-Style Macaroni Salad

serves 8

1 pound dry elbow macaroni, cooked, rinsed in cold water, and drained well

For the dressing

1½ cups mayonnaise

½ cup sour cream

2 tablespoons cider vinegar

1 tablespoon Dijon mustard

1 teaspoon sugar

½ cup finely diced celery

¼ cup minced red onion

½ cup sweet pickle relish

¼ cup finely grated carrot

2 tablespoons finely diced red bell pepper

¼ cup chopped parsley

½ teaspoon freshly ground black pepper

1½ teaspoons salt, or to taste

Whisk together all the dressing ingredients in a large mixing bowl, and add the drained pasta. Toss to combine thoroughly. Refrigerate for at least 2 hours before serving.

Note: Some of the minced vegetables can be reserved to scatter over the top for a more colorful presentation.

Ratatouille

1 red bell pepper, seeded and quartered

1 orange bell pepper, seeded and quartered

1 green bell pepper, seeded and quartered

1 pound 4 ounces eggplants, thickly sliced

2 tablespoons olive oil, plus extra for brushing

2 large onions, sliced

3 garlic cloves, finely chopped

3 medium zucchini, thickly sliced

5-6 medium tomatoes, peeled, seeded, and chopped

1½ teaspoons dried herbs

2 bay leaves

Salt and freshly ground pepper, to taste

Crusty bread, to serve

Preheat the broiler.

Put the bell pepper quarters, skin side up, on a baking sheet and broil until the skins are charred and blistered. Remove with tongs, put them into a plastic bag, tie the top, and let cool. Meanwhile, spread out the eggplant slices on the baking sheet, brush with oil, and broil for 5 minutes, until lightly browned. Turn, brush with oil, and broil for an additional 5 minutes, until lightly browned. Remove with tongs.

Remove the bell peppers from the bag and peel off the skins. Remove and discard the seeds and membranes and cut the flesh into strips. Dice the eggplant slices.

Heat the oil in a large pan or ovenproof casserole. Add the onions and cook over low heat, stirring occasionally, for 8–10 minutes, until lightly browned.

Add the garlic and zucchini, and cook, stirring occasionally, for an additional 10 minutes.

Stir in the bell peppers, eggplants, tomatoes, dried herbs, and bay leaves. Season to taste with salt and pepper, then cover and simmer over very low heat, stirring occasionally, for 25 minutes. Remove the lid and simmer, stirring occasionally, for an additional 25–35 minutes, until all the vegetables are tender.

Remove and discard the bay leaves. Serve the ratatouille immediately, if serving hot, or let cool, if serving at room temperature, accompanied by crusty bread.

Cheese & Chive Bread

serves 8

2 tablespoons butter, melted, plus extra for greasing

2 cups self-rising flour

1 teaspoon salt

1 teaspoon dry mustard

1 cup grated sharp cheese

2 tablespoons chopped fresh chives

1 egg, beaten

⅔ cup milk

Grease a 9-inch square cake pan and line the base with parchment paper.

Sift the flour, salt, and mustard into a large mixing bowl.

Reserve 3 tablespoons of the grated cheese for sprinkling over the top of the loaf before baking in the oven.

Stir the remaining cheese into the bowl, together with the chopped fresh chives. Mix well.

Add the beaten egg, melted butter, and milk and stir the mixture thoroughly.

Pour the mixture into the prepared pan and spread with a knife. Sprinkle with the reserved grated cheese.

Bake in a preheated oven, 375°F for about 30 minutes.

Let the bread cool slightly in the pan. Turn out onto a cooling rack to cool further before serving. Cut into triangles to serve.

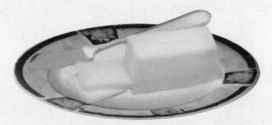

Arugula & Parmesan Salad with Pine Nuts

serves 4

2 handfuls of arugula leaves

1 small fennel bulb

5 tablespoons olive oil

2 tablespoons balsamic vinegar

½ cup Parmesan cheese, shavings

¼ cup pine nuts

Pinch of salt

Freshly ground black pepper

Wash the arugula, discarding any wilted leaves or coarse stems, and pat dry. Divide among 4 serving plates. Halve the fennel bulb and slice it finely. Arrange the sliced fennel over the arugula.

Whisk together the oil and vinegar with salt and pepper to taste. Drizzle a little of the dressing over each serving. Shave the Parmesan cheese thinly using a knife or vegetable peeler.

Toast the pine nuts in a dry skillet until golden brown. Top the salad with the Parmesan cheese shavings and toasted pine nuts. Serve immediately.

Macaroni & Cheese

6 tablespoons butter, divided

½ cup minced onion

3 tablespoons all-purpose flour

2¾ cups milk

½ teaspoon freshly chopped thyme leaves

Small pinch of nutmeg

Pinch of cayenne

Salt and pepper to taste

2 cups dry elbow macaroni

½ pound shredded cheddar cheese

¼ pound shredded Gruyere cheese, or other high-quality Swiss cheese

⅔ cup breadcrumbs

Pre-heat oven to 350°F.

Melt 4 tablespoons of the butter in a medium saucepan over medium heat. Sauté the onions in the butter for 4 to 5 minutes, until translucent. Do not brown. Stir in the flour, and cook for 2 minutes. Whisk in the cold milk, and cook, stirring, until the mixture comes to a simmer and thickens slightly. Turn off the heat and stir in the thyme, nutmeg, pinch of cayenne, salt and pepper to taste. Set aside until needed.

Boil the elbow macaroni in salted water, one minute less than the package directions state. Drain well and add to a large mixing bowl. Add the white sauce, and the cheeses, and fold with a spatula until thoroughly combined.

Transfer into a lightly buttered 9 x 13 inch baking dish. Melt 2 tablespoons of butter and mix with the breadcrumbs. Scatter evenly over the top of the casserole. Bake for 40 to 45 minutes, or until bubbly and golden brown.

Note: Cover loosely with foil towards the end of the cooking, if the top is getting too brown for your liking.

Baked Acorn Squash

serves 4

2 acorn squash

2 tablespoons freshly squeezed orange juice

1 tablespoon brown sugar

2 tablespoons unsalted butter

2 tablespoons real maple syrup

Salt and fresh ground black pepper to taste

Pre-heat oven to 400°F.

Cut the acorn squash in half lengthwise, and scoop the seeds and strings out of the cavity. Carefully score the inside of each squash with a sharp knife, making ⅛ inch deep cuts about ½ inch apart (refer to mouthwatering photo). Use a brush to paint each half with the orange juice. Sprinkle generously with salt. Bake for 30 minutes.

In a small saucepan, combine the brown sugar, butter, maple syrup and fresh ground black pepper. Bring to a boil, stir, and cook for one minute. Reserve.

Remove the squash from the oven, and spoon off any liquid that has accumulated in the cavities. Brush the glaze evenly over each, and bake for another 40 minutes, or until tender and caramelized on the edges. Allow to sit for 15 minutes before serving, possibly with a bit more salt sprinkled over.

For an extra nice glaze, baste squash with the syrup that collects in the cavity a few times while it's baking.

Braised Red Cabbage & Apples

serves 6

1 teaspoon of whole caraway seeds

1 tablespoon vegetable oil

1 red onion, halved and thinly sliced

2 tablespoons brown sugar

1 small red cabbage, shredded

2 apples, peeled and thinly sliced

2 tablespoons red wine

½ cup apple juice

2 tablespoons cider vinegar

Salt and freshly ground black pepper

1 teaspoon lemon juice

In a saucepan over medium heat, dry roast the caraway seeds for about 1 minute until they start to give off an aroma.

Heat the oil in a large pot over medium heat, add the onion, and sauté for 5 minutes until it becomes translucent. Add the brown sugar, stir, and add the cabbage and apples. Stir for a few minutes until the cabbage wilts. Add in the red wine, apple juice, and vinegar. Add the toasted caraway seeds and salt and pepper to taste. Bring the mixture to a boil, lower to a simmer, add the lemon juice, cover, and cook for 30 minutes.

Note: Braised cabbage is wonderful served with chicken, meat, or pork dishes.

Dinner Rolls

makes 16

¼ cup warm water

1 packet (2¼ teaspoons) dry active yeast

1 cup milk

3 tablespoons unsalted butter, room temperature

1 tablespoon sugar

1 tablespoon honey

¾ teaspoon salt

3 cups unbleached all-purpose white flour, plus more as needed

1 teaspoon vegetable oil

Pre-heat oven to 350°F.

Combine water and yeast in a large bowl. Whisk until dissolved, and set aside. Combine milk, butter, sugar, honey, and salt in another glass or plastic bowl. Microwave for one minute, or until milk is just warm. Set aside until butter is melted.

Add the flour to the bowl containing the water and yeast, followed by the milk mixture. Stir until a sticky dough forms. Turn dough out onto a well-floured work surface. Knead dough for about 6 minutes, adding enough flour, as needed to keep the dough from sticking to the surface, or your hands. Grease a large bowl with oil. Place the dough into the bowl and cover with a clean towel and leave to rise until it doubles in size, about 1½ hours.

Punch down the dough, and turn it out onto a lightly-floured surface. Shape into a square and cut into 16 equal-sized sections. Roll each piece into a ball. Line an 18 x 13 inch baking sheet with a silicon making mat. Place each ball, seam side down, about 2 inches apart on the baking sheet Put a teaspoon of flour in a fine mesh sieve and tap to dust the top of each roll with a little flour. Allow to rise for 40 minutes.

Bake on the center rack for about 25 minutes, until golden brown. Remove and let cool on a rack for 20 minutes before serving.

Scalloped Potatoes

serves 8

2 tablespoons butter, divided

1 tablespoon all-purpose flour

1 cup cream

2 cups milk

1 teaspoon salt

Pinch of nutmeg

Pinch of white pepper

4 springs fresh thyme

2 cloves garlic minced

4½ pounds russet potatoes, sliced thin

Salt and freshly ground black pepper to taste

½ cup grated Swiss gruyere or white cheddar

Pre-heat oven to 375°F.

Use half the butter to grease a 15 x 10 inch baking dish.

Melt the rest of the butter in a saucepan over medium heat. Whisk in the flour, and cook, stirring constantly, for 2 minutes. Whisk in the cream and milk, and bring to a simmer. Add the salt, nutmeg, white pepper, thyme, and garlic. Reduce heat to low, and simmer for 5 minutes. Remove the thyme springs; reserve.

Layer half the potatoes in the baking dish. Season generously with salt and freshly ground black pepper. Top with half of the milk mixture. Top with half the cheese. Repeat with the remaining potatoes, sauce, and cheese.

Bake for about 1 hour, or until the top is browned and the potatoes are tender. Let rest for 15 minutes before serving.

Caesar Salad with Garlic Croutons

serves 6 small or 12 large

For the dressing

2 egg yolks, from coddled eggs

2 large garlic cloves, minced

3 whole anchovy fillets

¾ cup mayonnaise

½ cup finely grated Parmigiano-Reggiano Parmesan cheese

⅓ cup olive oil

¼ cup freshly squeezed lemon juice

1 tablespoon cold water

1 teaspoon freshly ground black pepper, or to taste

Salt to taste

For the salads

6 hearts of romaine lettuce, torn or cut into 2 inch pieces, washed, dried thoroughly

¾ cup Caesar dressing, more as needed

4 cups Garlic Parmesan Croutons

1 cup shaved Parmesan cheese, more as needed

Freshly ground black pepper, to taste

For the dressing: To coddle eggs: Place 2 room temperature eggs in a small saucepan. Pour in boiling water until the eggs are covered. Leave for 1 minute, then drain and run under cold water until the eggs are cool enough to be handled. When cool separate the eggs and reserve the yolks.

Add the rest of the dressing ingredients to a blender, along with the egg yolks. Blend until smooth. Refrigerate until needed.

For the salads: Combine the romaine, croutons, and dressing in a large mixing bowl. Toss with tongs until the lettuce is completely coated with dressing. Divide onto chilled plates and top with the shaved Parmesan (a potato peeler works best for this), and freshly ground black pepper to taste. Serve immediately with extra dressing on the side.

Cheese & Ham Loaf

makes 1 loaf

6 tablespoons butter, diced, plus extra for greasing

1½ cups self-rising flour

1 teaspoon salt

2 teaspoons baking powder

1 teaspoon paprika

1¼ cups grated sharp cheese

½ cup chopped smoked ham

2 eggs, lightly beaten

⅓ cup milk

Preheat oven to 350°F.

Grease a 1 pound loaf pan with a little butter and line the base with parchment paper.

Sift the flour, salt, baking powder, and paprika into a large mixing bowl.

Rub in the butter with your fingertips until the mixture resembles fine breadcrumbs. Stir in the cheese and ham.

Add the beaten eggs and milk to the dry ingredients in the bowl and mix well.

Spoon the cheese and ham mixture into the prepared pan.

Bake for about 1 hour, or until the loaf is well risen.

Let the bread cool in the pan, then turn out, and transfer to a cooling rack to cool completely.

Cut the bread into thick slices to serve.

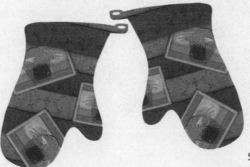

Green Bean Casserole

serves 6-8

1½ pounds green beans, trimmed, cut in thirds

1½ cups cream

½ cup chicken broth

1 clove garlic, minced fine

½ teaspoon salt

¼ teaspoon freshly ground black pepper

Pinch of nutmeg

One 6-ounce can French fried onions, divided

Pre-heat oven to 375°F.

Bring a pot of well-salted water to boil. Blanch the beans in the boiling water for 5 minutes. Drain very well and reserve.

Add the cream, broth, garlic, salt, and nutmeg to a small saucepan. Place over medium heat and cook, stirring occasionally, until the mixture comes to a simmer. Remove from heat and reserve.

Spread half the French fried onions in the bottom of a 2 quart casserole dish. Spread the beans evenly over the onions. Pour over the cream mixture. Use a fork to press the beans down into the cream. Top with the other half of the fried onions. Use a fork to flatten the top, pressing down firmly.

Bake for 25 to 30 minutes, or until the beans are very tender, and the casserole is browned and bubbling. Remove and let rest for 15 minutes before serving.

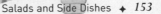

Waldorf Salad

serves 4

¾ cup raw walnut halves

3 apples, cored, cut into 1 inch chunks

1 cup green or red seedless grape halves

⅔ cup sliced celery, about ¼ inch thick

⅓ cup mayonnaise

2 tablespoons freshly squeezed lemon juice

1 tablespoon plain yogurt

½ teaspoon salt

Fresh ground black pepper to taste

1 small head butter lettuce

Pre-heat oven to 350°F.

Arrange walnuts on a baking sheet, and bake for 8 minutes. Let cool on a cutting board, roughly chop, and reserve.

Add the mayonnaise, lemon juice, yogurt, salt, and a few grinds of black pepper to a large mixing bowl. Whisk to combine thoroughly. Use a spatula to fold in the apples, grapes, celery, and walnuts. Mix until evenly coated with the dressing.

Lay down a few lettuce leaves on each plate and spoon the Waldorf salad over the top. Serve immediately.

Note: Try and use three different varieties of apple for an even more interesting salad.

Roasted Bell Pepper Salad

serves 4

4 large mixed red, green, and yellow bell peppers

4 tablespoons olive oil

1 large red onion, sliced

2 garlic cloves, crushed

4 tomatoes, peeled and chopped

pinch of sugar

1 teaspoon lemon juice

Salt and pepper

Trim and halve the bell peppers and remove the seeds.

Place the bell peppers, skin side up, under a preheated hot broiler. Cook until the skins char. Rinse under cold water and remove the skins.

Trim off any thick membranes and slice thinly.

Heat the oil in a skillet and fry the onion and garlic until softened. Then add the bell peppers and tomatoes and fry over low heat for 10 minutes.

Remove from the heat, add the sugar and lemon juice, and season to taste. Serve immediately or let cool (the flavors will develop as the salad cools).

Succulent Succotash

serves 8

1 tablespoon olive oil

½ tablespoon butter

½ yellow onion, diced

3 garlic cloves, minced

1 jalapeno or other small hot chile pepper, sliced

½ red bell pepper, diced

½ cup diced tomatoes, fresh if available

1 cup green beans, cut in ½ inch pieces

1½ cups fresh or frozen corn

1 cup frozen baby lima beans, thawed

1 cup cubed green zucchini

½ teaspoon ground cumin

Pinch of cayenne

¼ cup water

Salt and freshly ground black pepper to taste

Place a large skillet on medium heat, and add the olive oil and butter. When the butter foams up, add the onions and a big pinch of salt. Sauté for about 5 minutes, or until the onions begin to soften and turn golden.

Add the garlic, jalapeno, and bell pepper; sauté for 3 minutes. Add the rest of the ingredients, and cook, stirring occasionally until the vegetables are tender.

More liquid may be added if the mixture gets too dry. When done, taste for salt, and adjust the seasoning if needed. Serve immediately.

Turkey Couscous Salad

serves 4

1⅓ cups couscous

5 tablespoons olive oil

3 tablespoons red wine vinegar

12 ounces turkey breast fillet, cubed

1 teaspoon harissa paste

1⅓ cups diced zucchini

1 onion, chopped

½ cup chopped dried apricots

2 tablespoons toasted pine nuts

2 tablespoons chopped fresh cilantro

Salt and pepper

Chopped fresh cilantro, to garnish

Put the couscous into a large heatproof bowl. Pour in enough boiling water to cover. Stir well, cover, and let soak for about 15 minutes, until all the liquid has been absorbed. Use a fork to break up any clumps and stir in 3 tablespoons of the olive oil and the vinegar. Season with plenty of salt and pepper.

Heat the remaining oil in a large skillet and add the turkey and harissa paste. Cook, turning frequently, for 3 minutes, until the turkey is no longer pink. Add the zucchini and onion to the skillet and cook, stirring occasionally, for another 10–12 minutes, until the turkey and vegetables are golden brown and tender.

Stir the turkey and vegetables into the couscous with the apricots and pine nuts. Let cool for 10 minutes, then stir in the chopped cilantro and adjust the seasoning to taste. Serve piled into bowls and garnished with chopped cilantro.

Hush Puppies

makes 36

1¾ cups yellow
cornmeal

½ cup all-purpose
flour, sifted

1 small onion, finely
chopped

1 tablespoon granulated
white sugar

2 teaspoons baking
powder

½ teaspoon salt

¾ cup milk

1 egg, beaten

Vegetable oil for deep-
frying

Stir the cornmeal, flour, onion, sugar, baking powder, and salt together in a bowl and make a well in the center.

Beat the milk and egg together in a pitcher, then pour into the dry ingredients and stir until a thick batter forms.

Heat at least 2 inches of oil in a deep skillet or pan over high heat until the temperature reaches 350°F to 375°F, or until a cube of bread browns in 30 seconds.

Drop in as many teaspoonfuls of the batter as will fit without overcrowding the skillet and cook, stirring constantly, until the Hush Puppies puff up and turn golden.

Remove the Hush Puppies from the oil with a slotted spoon and drain on paper towels. Reheat the oil, if necessary, and cook the remaining batter. Serve hot.

Cobb Salad

serves 4

8 slices bacon

4 large handfuls mixed baby greens, or other lettuce, torn into bite-size pieces

3 hard-boiled eggs, peeled, chopped

4 cups cooked chicken, cubed

2 avocados, peeled, pitted, cubed

1 cup cherry tomatoes, halved

½ cup Roquefort cheese, crumbled

½ teaspoon Dijon mustard

¼ cup red wine vinegar

1 teaspoon Worcestershire sauce

1 clove garlic, crushed into a paste

¼ teaspoon salt

¼ teaspoon fresh ground black pepper

⅓ cup olive oil

Cook the bacon until crisp, drain on paper towels, and when cool enough to handle, crumble and set aside.

Arrange a bed of lettuce in shallow bowls. Arrange the eggs, bacon, chicken, avocados, tomatoes, and Roquefort cheese in rows on top of the lettuce, covering the surface completely.

In a bowl, whisk together the mustard, vinegar, Worcestershire, garlic, salt, and pepper. Slowly drizzle in the olive oil, whisking constantly, to form the dressing.

Drizzle the dressing evenly over the salad, and serve immediately.

Creamy Corn Custard

serves 8

3 cups corn kernels, fresh, or thawed frozen

1½ cups heavy cream

½ cup milk

1¼ teaspoons salt

Pinch of cayenne

3 egg yolks

4 eggs

Butter as needed

8 (6 ounces) oven-proof ramekins, buttered

Pre-heat oven to 325°F.

Add the corn, cream, milk, salt, and cayenne to a saucepan. Bring to a simmer over medium heat. Turn off heat and remove to cool slightly. Carefully pour into a blender and puree until very smooth. Reserve.

Add the eggs and egg yolks to a mixing bowl and whisk for 30 seconds. Slowly, a cup at a time, stir in the warm corn custard mixture. When everything is combined, ladle the mixture into 8 well buttered, 6 ounce ramekins.

Fill a roasting pan or casserole dish with 1-inch of hot water and place in the filled ramekins. Bake for 35 minutes, or until the corn custard is just set. Remove from the baking dish and let cool for 15 minutes before serving.

May be eaten out of the ramekins – or run a paring knife around the inside, and turn over on to a plate for a "fancier" presentation.

Cajun Chicken Salad

4 skinless, boneless chicken

4 teaspoons Cajun seasoning

2 teaspoons corn oil

1 ripe mango, peeled, pitted, and cut into thick slices

7 ounces mixed salad greens

1 red onion, halved and thinly sliced

1¼ cups diced, cooked beets

½ cup radishes, sliced

½ cup walnut halves

2 tablespoons sesame seeds

Dressing

4 tablespoons walnut oil

1–2 teaspoons whole-grain mustard

1 tablespoon lemon juice

Salt and pepper

Make 3 diagonal slashes across each chicken breast. Put the chicken into a shallow dish and sprinkle all over with the Cajun seasoning. Cover and let chill for at least 30 minutes.

When ready to cook, brush a stove-top grill pan with the corn oil. Heat over high heat until very hot and a few drops of water sprinkled into the pan sizzle immediately. Add the chicken and cook for 7–8 minutes on each side, or until thoroughly cooked. If still slightly pink in the center, cook a little longer. Remove the chicken and set aside.

Add the mango slices to the pan and cook for 2 minutes on each side. Remove and set aside.

Meanwhile, arrange the salad greens in a serving bowl and sprinkle over the onion, beets, radishes, and walnut halves.

To make the dressing, put the walnut oil, mustard, lemon juice, and salt and pepper to taste in a screw-top jar and shake until well blended. Pour over the salad and sprinkle with the sesame seeds.

Cut the reserved chicken into thick slices. Arrange the mango and the salad on a serving plate and top with the chicken breast and a few of the salad greens.

Cheesy Broccoli Gratin

serves 6

1/4 cup butter

1/4 cup flour

2 cups cold milk

Pinch of nutmeg

Pinch of cayenne

1 teaspoon fresh thyme leaves, chopped (optional)

1 cup extra-sharp cheddar cheese, shredded

1/2 teaspoon salt, or to taste

2 pounds fresh broccoli crowns, cut into 2 inch pieces

1/2 cup plain breadcrumbs

2 tablespoons melted butter

2 tablespoons grated Parmesan cheese

Pre-heat oven to 375°F.

Melt the butter in a saucepan over medium heat, and add the flour. Cook, stirring, for about 3 minutes (the mixture should begin to smell like cooked piecrust). Slowly whisk in the cold milk. Continue whisking until there are no visible lumps. Add the nutmeg, cayenne, and thyme. The sauce will thicken as it comes back to a simmer. Reduce the heat to low, and simmer, stirring occasionally, for 10 minutes.

Turn off the heat, and stir in the cheese. When all the cheese has melted into the sauce, season with salt, and reserve until needed.

Note: Sauce may be strained if you are concerned about lumps.

Bring a pot of salted water to a rapid boil. Add the broccoli and cook for about 5 minutes, or just until the stem ends begin to get tender. Do not overcook, as the broccoli will cook further in the oven. Drain very well (otherwise the gratin will be watery). Transfer to a large mixing bowl.

Pour over the cheese sauce, and fold with a spatula until the broccoli is completely coated with the sauce. Transfer into a lightly buttered 2 quart casserole dish, using the spatula to distribute evenly. In a small bowl combine breadcrumbs, butter, and Parmesan. Sprinkle evenly over the top, and oven-bake for 25 minutes, or until the top is browned and bubbly.

Potato and Egg Salad

serves 10

4 pounds russet potatoes, peeled, quartered

3 hard-boiled eggs, chopped

1 cup diced celery

⅓ cup minced green onions, white and light green parts only

1¼ cup mayonnaise

2 tablespoons cider vinegar

1 tablespoon Dijon mustard

1½ teaspoons salt

½ teaspoon sugar

¼ teaspoon freshly ground black pepper

pinch cayenne pepper, optional

Boil potatoes in salted water until just tender, drain well, and let cool to room temperature. Cut into 1 inch pieces and add to a large bowl. Add the eggs and celery.

In a small mixing bowl combine the rest of the ingredients. Pour over the potato mixture, and use a spatula to thoroughly combine.

Chill in the refrigerator for at least one hour before serving.

Roasted Vegetables

¼ cup olive oil

1 garlic clove, peeled, left whole, but crushed slightly

2 large red bell peppers, seeded, cut into ½ inch strips

4 green zucchini, halved, then cut lengthwise into quarters

1 red onion, peeled, cut in eighths

2 pounds Yukon gold potatoes, cut in wedges

4 carrots, peeled, cut in thirds, then into ½ inch sticks

½ lemon, juiced

1 teaspoon fresh rosemary spring, leaves picked

2 tablespoons fresh chopped parsley

Salt and fresh ground black pepper to taste

Pre-heat oven to 450°F.

In a small saucepan, warm the oil and garlic over low heat, until the garlic begins to bubble. Turn off the heat and allow to sit for 30 minutes to infuse the oil. Remove the garlic clove and reserve the oil.

Add the remaining ingredients to a large mixing bowl, along with the garlic oil. Toss to coat completely.

Arrange in a single layer on one or more foil lined baking sheets. Roast for 20 minutes in pre-heated oven. Remove and stir the vegetables so they cook evenly. Put back in and roast for another 25 to 35 minutes, or until the vegetable are tender and the edges are browned.

Season with additional salt and fresh ground black pepper to taste. Serve hot, sprinkled with freshly chopped parsley.

Southwest Corn Salad

3 tablespoons olive oil

3 cups fresh corn kernels, about 6 ears

One 15-ounce can black beans, well rinsed and drained

1 red bell pepper, diced small

1 orange bell pepper, diced small

1 jalapeno pepper, seeded, minced

4 thinly sliced green onions

1 clove garlic, crushed, finely minced

2 tablespoons chopped cilantro leaves

½ teaspoon ground cumin

¼ teaspoon chipotle pepper, or to taste

3 tablespoons fresh lime juice

1 tablespoon rice vinegar

1 teaspoon sugar

1 teaspoon salt

Heat the olive oil in a large nonstick pan over medium-high heat. Add the corn and sauté, stirring, for about 3 to 4 minutes.

Turn off the pan and transfer corn into a large mixing bowl. Add the rest of the ingredients and toss to combine thoroughly.

Refrigerate for at least 4 hours before serving. Toss well, and taste and adjust for salt and spice before serving.

Cornbread

serves 6

½ cup (1 stick) unsalted butter, melted

⅔ cup sugar

2 large eggs

1 cup buttermilk

½ teaspoon baking soda

½ teaspoon salt

1 cup all-purpose flour

1 cup yellow cornmeal

Extra butter to grease the pan

Pre-heat oven to 375°F.

In a large mixing bowl, whisk together the melted butter and sugar. Add the eggs; whisk until combined. Add the buttermilk and baking soda; whisk to combine. Add the flour, cornmeal, and salt. Using a spatula stir until just blended. Do not mix any longer than necessary.

Lightly grease a 10 inch cast iron skillet with butter. Pour in the batter and bake for about 35 minutes, or until a toothpick inserted in the center comes out clean.

Let cool for at least 15 minutes before trying to cut.

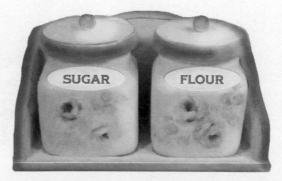

Warm Bacon & Egg Salad

2 romaine lettuce hearts, coarsely torn

4 eggs

2 tablespoons sunflower oil

2 thick slices of bread, crusts removed and cubed

1⅓ cups cubed smoked bacon

12 cherry tomatoes, halved

Dressing

2 tablespoons extra virgin olive oil

1 tablespoon red wine vinegar

1 teaspoon Dijon mustard

Pepper

To make the dressing, put all the ingredients into a small screw-top jar and shake until well blended. Put the lettuce leaves in a salad bowl.

Place the eggs in a saucepan and cover with cold water. Bring to the boil and boil for 4 minutes. Drain and plunge the eggs into cold water for 2 minutes. Peel off the shells and cut into quarters.

To make croutons, heat the sunflower oil in a large skillet and fry the bread cubes for 3–4 minutes, turning frequently until golden brown. Remove with a slotted spoon and set aside.

Add the bacon cubes to the pan and fry over medium–high heat until crisp and golden. Add the tomatoes and dressing to the pan and cook for an additional minute.

Gently toss the bacon, tomatoes, and dressing into the salad leaves. Add the quartered eggs and scatter over the croutons. Serve immediately.

Buttermilk Biscuits

makes 12-14

2 cups all-purpose flour

2 teaspoons baking powder

¼ teaspoon baking soda

1 teaspoon salt

7 tablespoons unsalted butter, cut into thin slices, chilled in freezer

¾ cup cold buttermilk

Pre-heat oven to 425°F.

In a mixing bowl, whisk together the dry ingredients to thoroughly combine. Cut in the ice cold butter slices using a wire pastry blender, until the mixture has the texture of coarse crumbs.

Make a well in the center and pour in the cold buttermilk. Stir the dry ingredients into the buttermilk with a fork until a loose, sticky dough is formed. Stop as soon as the mixture comes together. Form into a ball and turn the dough out onto a floured work surface.

With floured hands, pat the dough into a rectangle (about 8 x 4 inch-thick). Fold dough in thirds (like folding a letter-sized piece of paper). Repeat this process twice more.

On a lightly-floured surface, roll or pat the dough out about ½ inch thick. Cut with a round biscuit cutter, and place on a parchment or silicon mat-lined baking sheet, a few inches apart. You can gather up any extra dough after cutting, and repeat to get a few more biscuits, although the texture may suffer from the extra working.

Make a slight depression in the center of each biscuit with your thumb (to help them rise evenly). Brush the tops lightly with buttermilk. Bake for about 15 minutes, or until risen and golden brown. Cool on a rack for 10 minutes before serving.

Shopping List:

Roasted Red Potato Salad

serves 6

2½ pounds small red potatoes, washed

Salt to taste

2 cloves garlic, finely minced

1 teaspoon Dijon mustard

Pinch of cayenne

¼ cup white wine vinegar

1 tablespoon chopped Italian parsley

1 tablespoon chopped tarragon

1 tablespoon chopped chives

1 teaspoon minced thyme leaves

⅔ cup olive oil

Freshly ground black pepper to taste

Pre-heat oven to 400°F.

Place the potatoes in a roasting pan. Bake for 25 to 30 minutes, or until tender (time will vary depending on size).

While the potatoes are in the oven, make the dressing. Add the garlic, Dijon, cayenne, and vinegar to a large mixing bowl. Whisk in the oil, very slowly at first, in a steady stream until incorporated.

When the cooked potatoes are just cool enough to handle, cut in halves or quarters. Add and toss the warm potatoes in the dressing, along with salt and fresh ground black pepper to taste. Let sit for 15 minutes. Add the herbs and toss again.

Cover and refrigerate for at least 2 hours or overnight. Toss well before serving, and taste for salt and pepper. Additional fresh herbs can be sprinkled over the top if desired.

Country Loaf

serves 6

1 packet (2¼ teaspoons) dry active yeast

¼ teaspoon sugar

1¼ cup warm water

3 cups unbleached white bread flour, divided

1 teaspoon salt

1 teaspoon vegetable oil

Cornmeal as needed

Pre-heat oven to 425°F.

Add the yeast, sugar, warm water, and 1½ cups of the flour to a large mixing bowl. Stir together until smooth, cover with a towel and leave in a warm spot (like an oven with the light on) for 2 hours.

Add 1 more cup of flour, and the salt, and stir to form a sticky dough. Turn dough out on a well-floured work surface. Knead dough for about 10 minutes, adding the last ½ cup of flour, but only as needed to keep the dough from sticking to the surface, or your hands. You want a very soft, supple, elastic dough, so use the flour very sparingly.

Grease a large bowl with vegetable oil. Form the dough into a ball, and place into the bowl; turn over a few times so the dough is lightly oiled. Cover the bowl with a towel and leave to rise in warm spot until it doubles in size, about 2 hours.

Prep a sheet pan by generously sprinkling with cornmeal. Punch down the dough, and turn it out onto a lightly-floured surface. Shape into an oval loaf and place on the baking sheet, seam side down. Dust the top of the loaf lightly with flour and cover with a light, dry towel. Allow to rise for 1 hour in a warm spot.

Place a cake pan, half-filled with water on the bottom rack of the oven. When the oven is hot, remove the towel, and bake the bread on the middle rack for 45 minutes or until browned. Allow to cool completely on a rack before slicing.

Glazed Yams

serves 6-8

1 lemon, juiced

2½ pounds Garnet, or other orange-fleshed yams

2 tablespoons unsalted butter

¼ cup packed brown sugar

½ teaspoon salt, or to taste

Pinch cayenne pepper

Pre-heat oven to 350°F.

Add the lemon juice to a large mixing bowl. Peel yams, cut in 1 inch cubes, and toss with the lemon juice.

Melt the butter in a large skillet over medium-high heat. Add the yams and lemon juice, brown sugar, salt, and cayenne. Cook, stirring, for about 5 to 7 minutes, until a sticky syrup is formed and the edges of the yams begin to caramelize.

Remove from heat and transfer into a lightly buttered, oven-proof baking dish. Bake for 20 to 25 minutes or until tender. Serve hot.

Garlic & Herb Steak Fries

serves 8

4 medium russet potatoes, scrubbed and rinsed

3 tablespoons olive oil

4 cloves garlic, minced and mashed against the cutting board with the flat of a knife

½ teaspoon dried rosemary, crushed fine

½ teaspoon dried oregano

½ teaspoon dried thyme

½ teaspoon paprika

½ teaspoon freshly ground black pepper

1 teaspoon salt

Pre-heat oven to 425°F.

Cut each potato in half lengthwise. Cut each half, lengthwise, into 4 equally sized wedges. Add the potato wedges to a large mixing bowl with the rest of the ingredients. Toss meticulously to coat the potatoes evenly.

Line a sheet pan with foil. Place the potato wedges, skin side down, on the foil. Be sure to space evenly, so they cook uniformly.

Bake for 35 to 40 minutes, or until well-browned, crusty-edged, and tender. Serve immediately, sprinkled with more salt if desired.

4

Something Sweet

Cinnamon Swirl Sour Cream Bundt Cake

serves 6-8

2½ cups all-purpose flour

1 teaspoon baking powder

1 teaspoon baking soda

½ teaspoon salt

¾ cup (1½ sticks) unsalted butter

1½ cups sugar

3 large eggs

1 cup sour cream

1 teaspoon vanilla extract

½ cup chopped walnuts, optional

For the swirl

1 tablespoon ground cinnamon

3 tablespoons brown sugar

2 tablespoons sugar

For the glaze

1 cup powdered sugar

About 1½ tablespoons milk

1 teaspoon ground cinnamon, or to taste

Pre-heat oven to 350°F.

Whisk together the flour, baking powder, baking soda, and salt in a mixing bowl for a minute; reserve until needed.

Cream the butter and sugar together until light and fluffy. Beat in the eggs one at a time, mixing thoroughly before adding the next. Beat in the sour cream and vanilla until combined. Add the flour mixture, stirring just until combined. Stir in the walnuts.

Butter a 10 inch bundt pan, and lightly dust with flour. Pour half the batter into the pan and spread evenly. Mix the ingredients for the swirl in a small bowl. Sprinkle evenly around the center of the batter. Cover with the rest of the batter.

Bake for 50 minutes, or until a toothpick inserted in the center comes out clean. Let cool 20 minutes before removing from the pan.

For the glaze: Add the powdered sugar to a small mixing bowl, stir in enough milk to create a thick, but pourable glaze. Stir in the cinnamon to taste. Drizzle over the top of the cake. Once the icing is set, slice and serve with lots of hot coffee.

Double Fudge Brownies

makes 9

1¼ cups bittersweet baking chocolate, broken into small pieces

⅓ cup butter, sliced into pieces

1 cup sugar

¼ teaspoon salt

2 tablespoons water

2 large eggs

1 teaspoon vanilla extract

¾ cup all-purpose flour

½ cup chopped walnuts (optional)

Pre-heat oven to 325°F.

Place the chocolate, butter, sugar, salt, and water in small saucepan over a very low flame. Heat, stirring often, until the chocolate and butter are melted.

Pour into a mixing bowl. Stir in the eggs, one at a time. Stir in the vanilla. Stir in the flour. Stir in the nuts, if using.

Pour into a lightly greased 8 inch-square baking dish.

Bake for 35 minutes. Cool completely before cutting into 9 squares.

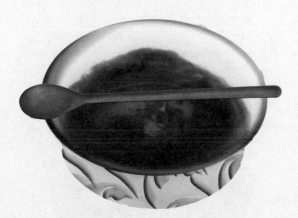

Peach Cobbler

serves 4-6

For the filling

6 peaches, peeled and sliced

4 tablespoons sugar

½ tablespoon lemon juice

1½ teaspoons cornstarch

½ teaspoon almond or vanilla essence

Vanilla or pecan ice cream

For the pie topping

1½ cups all-purpose flour

½ cup sugar

1½ teaspoons baking powder

½ teaspoon salt

6 tablespoons diced butter

1 egg

6 tablespoons milk

Pre-heat oven to 425°F.

Place the peaches in a 9 inch square ovenproof dish. Add the sugar, lemon juice, cornflour and almond essence and toss together. Bake in pre-heated oven for 20 minutes.

Meanwhile, to make the topping, sift the flour, all but 2 tablespoons of the sugar, the baking powder and the s alt into a bowl. Rub in the butter with the fingertips until the mixture resembles breadcrumbs. Mix the egg and 5 tablespoons of the milk in a jug, then mix into the dry ingredients with a fork until a soft, sticky dough forms. If the dough seems too dry, stir in the extra tablespoon of milk.

Reduce the oven temperature to 400°F. Remove the peaches from the oven and drop spoonfuls of the topping over the surface, without smoothing. Sprinkle with the remaining sugar, return to the oven and bake for a further 15 minutes or until the topping is golden brown and firm— the topping will spread as it cooks. Serve hot or at room temperature, with ice cream.

Magic Lemon Sponge Cake

serves 4

¾ cup sugar

3 eggs, separated

1¼ cups whole milk

3 tablespoons self-rising flour, sifted

⅔ cup lemon juice

Confectioners' sugar, for dusting

Using an electric mixer, beat the sugar with the egg yolks in a bowl. Gradually beat in the milk, followed by the flour and lemon juice.

Whisk the egg whites in a separate grease-free bowl until stiff. Fold half the whites into the yolk mixture, using a spatula in a figure-eight movement, then fold in the remainder. Try not to knock out the air.

Pour the mixture into a heatproof bowl and cover with aluminum foil. Stand the bowl on a trivet in the slow cooker and pour in enough boiling water to come about one-third of the way up the side of the bowl. Cover and cook on high for

2½ hours, until the mixture has set and the sauce and sponge have separated.

Carefully remove the bowl from the slow cooker and discard the foil. Transfer to warmed bowls, lightly dust with confectioners' sugar, and serve immediately.

New York Cheesecake with Fruit Sauce

serves 8-10

½ cup (1 stick) butter

1¾ cups finely crushed graham crackers

1 tablespoon granulated white sugar

2 pounds cream cheese

1¼ cups sugar

2 tablespoons all purpose flour

1 teaspoon vanilla extract

Finely grated zest of 1 orange

Finely grated zest of 1 lemon

3 eggs

2 egg yolks

1¼ cups heavy cream

For the sauce

1 cup berries, such as blackberries or raspberries

2 tablespoons water

2 to 3 tablespoons sugar

2 tablespoons fruit liqueur, such as crème de cassis or crème de framboise

Pre-heat the oven to 350°F.

Place a small saucepan over low heat, melt the butter and remove from heat. Stir in crushed crackers and the 1 tablespoon sugar. Mix. Press the cracker mixture into bottom of a 9 inch cake pan. Place in an oven and bake for 10 minutes. Remove and cool.

Increase oven temperature to 400°F. With an electric food mixer beat cream cheese until creamy and gradually add sugar and flour and beat until smooth. Beat in the vanilla extract, orange and lemon zest, then one at a time beat in the eggs and egg yolks. Finally beat in the cream. The mixture should be light and whippy.

Grease the sides of the cake pan and pour in the filling. Transfer to the pre-heated oven and bake for 15 minutes. Reduce heat to 200°F. and bake for an additional 30 minutes. Turn the oven off and leave to cool for 2 hours. Cover and refrigerate overnight.

For the sauce: Put all the ingredients into a small, heavy-bottomed pan and heat gently, until the sugar has dissolved and the fruit juices run. Process to a paste in a food processor, then push through a non-metallic strainer into a serving bowl to remove the seeds. Add more sugar if necessary and serve warm or cold.

Boston Cream Pie

serves 6-8

1 (18.25 ounces) package white or yellow cake mix, prepared according to directions

For the pastry cream

1 cup whipping cream

1 cup whole milk

1 tablespoon butter

7 tablespoons sugar

2 tablespoons cornstarch

3 large eggs

1½ teaspoons pure vanilla extract

Pinch of salt

For the chocolate topping (called a ganache

¾ cup high-quality bittersweet chocolate, chopped

½ cup heavy cream

1 teaspoon butter

For the pastry cream: Combine the sugar, cornstarch, and eggs in a mixing bowl; whisk vigorously until the mixture is light and creamy; set aside.

Bring the cream, milk, and butter to a boil in a small saucepan over medium-high heat. Quickly whisk in the egg mixture, and boil, stirring constantly, for exactly one minute. The mixture should become very thick, very quickly. Remove from heat and strain into a clean bowl. Cover the surface with plastic wrap, and let cool at room temp for 20 minutes. Place in the fridge until completely cold; overnight is best. Before using, whisk in the vanilla, and season with a pinch of salt to taste.

Place one cake down on a cake plate, top with the pastry cream and lay the other cake gently on top.

For the chocolate topping: Place the chopped chocolate in a small heatproof bowl and set aside. Bring the cream and butter to a simmer over medium-high heat, then quickly pour over the chocolate. Let sit undisturbed for 3 minutes, then gently whisk to combine.

The chocolate mixture will slowly thicken as it cools. When the mixture has thickened slightly, yet is still just thin enough to pour, spread evenly over the top of the cake. Start in the center and slowly work the chocolate toward the edges. Refrigerate until the chocolate has firmed up completely before slicing and serving.

Creme Brulee

1 vanilla bean
4 cups heavy cream
6 egg yolks
½ cup sugar
½ cup firmly packed
light brown sugar

Using a sharp knife, split the vanilla bean in half lengthwise, scrape the seeds into a pan, and add the bean. Pour in the cream and bring just to a boil, stirring constantly. Remove from the heat, cover, and let steep for 20 minutes.

Whisk together the egg yolks and superfine sugar in a bowl until thoroughly mixed. Remove and discard the vanilla bean from the pan, then whisk the cream into the egg yolk mixture. Strain the mixture into a large pitcher.

Divide the mixture among 6 individual baking dishes and cover with aluminum foil. Stand the dishes on a trivet in the slow cooker and pour in enough boiling water to come about halfway up the sides of the dishes. Cover and cook on low for 3–3½ hours, until just set. Remove the slow cooker pot from the base unit and let cool completely, then remove the dishes and chill in the refrigerator for at least 4 hours.

Preheat the broiler. Sprinkle the brown sugar evenly over the surface of each dessert, then cook under the preheated broiler for 30–60 seconds, until the sugar has melted and caramelized. Alternatively, you can use a cook's blowtorch. Return the dishes to the refrigerator and chill for an additional hour before serving.

Almond Sponge Cake

serves 4

Unsalted butter, for greasing

10–12 ladyfingers

1¼ cups milk

2 eggs

2 tablespoons sugar

½ cup chopped blanched almonds

4–5 drops of almond extract

Sherry sauce

1 tablespoon sugar

3 egg yolks

⅔ cup sweet sherry

Grease a 2½-cup heatproof bowl. Line the bowl with the ladyfingers, cutting them to fit and placing them cut-sides down and sugar-coated sides outward. Cover the bottom of the bowl with some of the trimmings.

Pour the milk into a pan and bring just to a boil, then remove from the heat. Beat together the eggs and sugar in a heatproof bowl until combined, then stir in the milk. Stir in the almonds and almond extract.

Carefully pour the mixture into the prepared bowl, making sure that the ladyfingers stay in place, and cover the bowl with aluminum foil. Stand the bowl on a trivet in the slow cooker and pour in enough boiling water to come about halfway up the side of the dish. Cover and cook on high for 3–3½ hours, until set.

Shortly before serving, make the sherry sauce. Put the sugar, egg yolks, and sherry into a heatproof bowl. Set the bowl over a pan of simmering water, without letting the bottom of the bowl touch the surface of the water. Whisk well until the mixture thickens, but do not let it boil. Remove from the heat.

Carefully remove the bowl from the slow cooker and discard the foil. Let stand for 2–3 minutes, then turn out onto a warmed serving plate. Pour the sherry sauce around it and serve immediately.

Blackberry & Apple Loaf Cake

serves 8-10

1 tablespoon butter, for greasing

2 large baking apples peeled and diced

3 tablespoons lemon juice

2 cups whole wheat flour

2½ teaspoon baking powder

1 teaspoon ground cinnamon, plus extra for dusting

1 cup blackberries, thawed if frozen, plus extra, for decorating

1 cup firmly packed light brown sugar

1 egg, beaten lightly

¾ cup lowfat plain yogurt

¼ cup brown sugar lumps, crushed lightly

One small sliced apple, for decorating

Preheat the oven to 375°F.

Grease a 9 x 5 x 4-inch loaf pan and line with parchment paper.

Core, peel, and finely dice the cooking apples. Place them in a pan with the lemon juice, bring to a boil, cover, and simmer for 10 minutes, until soft. Beat well. Set aside to cool.

Sift the flour, baking powder, and cinnamon into a bowl, adding any bran that remains in the sifter. Stir in ⅔ cup of the blackberries and the sugar. Make a well in the center of the ingredients and add the egg, yogurt, and cooled apple paste. Mix until thoroughly blended. Spoon the mixture into the prepared loaf pan and level over the top with a spatula.

Sprinkle with the remaining blackberries, pressing them down into the cake batter, and top the batter with the crushed sugar lumps.

Bake for 40–45 minutes until a tester inserted in the middle comes out clean. Cool in the pan.

Turn the cake out and peel away the parchment paper. Serve dusted with cinnamon and decorated with the remaining blackberries and apple slices.

Chocolate Mousse

1¼ cups light cream

1¼ cups milk

1 cup bittersweet chocolate, broken into small pieces

1 extra large egg

4 egg yolks

4 tablespoons sugar

⅔ cup heavy cream chocolate curls, to decorate

Pour the light cream and milk into a pan and add the chocolate. Set the pan over very low heat and stir until the chocolate has melted and the mixture is smooth. Remove from the heat and let cool for 10 minutes.

Beat together the egg, egg yolks, and sugar in a bowl until combined. Gradually stir in the chocolate mixture until thoroughly blended. Strain into a pitcher.

Divide the mixture among 6 individual baking dishes and cover with aluminum foil. Stand the dishes on a trivet in the slow cooker and pour in enough boiling water to come about halfway up the sides of the dishes. Cover and cook on low for 3–3½ hours, until just set. Remove the slow cooker pot from the base unit and let cool completely, then remove the dishes and chill in the refrigerator for at least 4 hours.

Whip the heavy cream in a bowl until it holds soft peaks. Top each chocolate mousse with cream and decorate with chocolate curls. Serve immediately.

Poached Peaches in Marsala Wine

serves 4-6

⅔ cup water, plus 2 tablespoons

⅔ cup Marsala wine

4 tablespoons sugar

1 vanilla bean, split lengthwise

6 peaches, cut into wedges and pitted or 12 apricots, halved and pitted

2 teaspoons cornstarch

Strained plain yogurt, to serve

Pour the ⅔ cup of water and the Marsala wine into a pan and add the sugar and vanilla bean. Set the pan over low heat and stir until the sugar has dissolved, then bring to a boil without stirring. Remove from the heat.

Put the peaches into the slow cooker and pour the syrup over them. Cover and cook on high for 1–1½ hours, until the fruit is tender.

Using a slotted spoon, gently transfer the peaches to a serving dish. Remove the vanilla bean from the slow cooker and scrape the seeds into the syrup with the point of a knife. Discard the bean. Stir the cornstarch to a paste with the 2 tablespoons of water in a small bowl, then stir into the syrup. Re-cover and cook on high for 15 minutes, stirring occasionally.

Spoon the syrup over the fruit and let cool. Serve warm or chill in the refrigerator for 2 hours before serving with yogurt.

Apple Crumble

½ cup all-purpose flour

½ cup rolled oats

⅔ cup light brown sugar

½ teaspoon freshly grated nutmeg

½ teaspoon ground cinnamon

1 cup (2 sticks) softened unsalted butter

4 baking apples, peeled, cored, and sliced

4–5 tablespoons apple juice

Strained plain yogurt, to serve

Sift the flour into a bowl and stir in the oats, sugar, nutmeg, and cinnamon. Add the butter and mix in with a pastry blender or the tines of a fork.

Place the apple slices in the bottom of the slow cooker and add the apple juice. Sprinkle the flour mixture evenly over them.

Cover and cook on low for 5½ hours. Serve hot, warm, or cold with yogurt.

Pound Cake with Orange Glaze

serves 6

2 cups all-purpose flour

1 teaspoon baking powder

¼ teaspoon baking soda

½ teaspoon salt

2 sticks (1 cup) unsalted butter

1¼ cups white sugar

1 tablespoon grated lemon zest

1 tablespoon grated orange zest

4 eggs

½ cup buttermilk

For the glaze

1 cup confectioner's sugar

1½ tablespoons fresh orange juice, or as needed

1 tablespoon freshly grated orange zest

Pre-heat oven to 325°F.

Butter one loaf pan, and dust with flour. Set aside. Sift together the flour, baking powder, baking soda, and salt in a mixing bowl. Set aside.

In a large mixing bowl, use an electric mixer to beat the butter, sugar, and zests until very light and creamy. Beat in the eggs, one at time, beating very thoroughly after each addition. Use a spatula to mix in flour alternately with the buttermilk, ending with flour. Scrape the batter into the prepared loaf pan.

Bake for 1 hour to 1 hour 15 minutes, or until a toothpick inserted in the center comes out clean. Remove and let rest for 15 minutes, then turn onto a cooling rack. Let cool 15 more minutes before glazing.

Stir together the orange glaze ingredients, adding enough orange juice to get a smooth spreadable consistency. Apply to the top of the warm cake. Let the pound cake cool completely before slicing.

Sweet Potato Pie

serves 8-10

For the pie dough

1¼ cups all-purpose flour, plus extra for dusting

½ teaspoon salt

¼ teaspoon sugar

1½ tablespoons butter, diced

3 tablespoons vegetable shortening, diced

2 to 2½ tablespoons ice-cold water

For the filling

1 pound 2 ounces orange-fleshed sweet potatoes, scrubbed

3 extra-large eggs, beaten

½ cup firmly packed brown sugar

1½ cups canned evaporated milk

3 tablespoons butter, melted

2 teaspoons vanilla extract

1 teaspoon ground cinnamon

1 teaspoon ground nutmeg or freshly grated nutmeg

½ teaspoon salt

Freshly whipped cream, to serve

Pre heat oven to 425°F.

To make the pie dough, sift the flour, salt, and sugar into a bowl. Add the butter and vegetable shortening to the bowl and rub in with the fingertips until fine crumbs form. Sprinkle over 2 tablespoons of the water and mix with a fork until a soft dough forms. Add ½ tablespoon of water if the dough is too dry. Wrap in plastic wrap and chill for at least 1 hour.

Meanwhile, bring a large pan of water to a boil over high heat. Add the sweet potatoes and cook for 15 minutes. Drain, then cool them under cold running water. When cool, peel, then mash. Put the sweet potatoes into a separate bowl and beat in the eggs and sugar until very smooth. Beat in the remaining ingredients, except the whipped cream, then set aside until required.

Roll out the dough on a lightly floured counter into a thin 11 inch circle and use to line a 9 inch pie plate, about 1½ inches high. Trim off the excess dough and press the floured tines of a fork around the edge. Prick the base of the pastry shell all over with the fork and place crumpled kitchen foil in the center. Bake in the oven for 12 minutes, or until lightly golden. Remove the pastry shell from the oven, take out the foil, pour the filling into the shell, and return to the oven for an additional 10 minutes. Reduce the oven temperature to 325°F and bake for a further 35 minutes, or until a knife inserted into the center comes out clean.

Let cool on a cooling rack. Serve warm or at room temperature with whipped cream.

Lemon Meringue Pie

serves 8-10

Butter, for greasing

9 ounces ready-made unsweetened pie dough, thawed if frozen

All-purpose flour, for dusting

3 tablespoons cornstarch

½ cup sugar

Grated rind of 3 lemons

1¼ cups cold water

⅔ cup lemon juice

3 egg yolks

½ stick unsalted butter, diced

For the meringue

3 egg whites

1 cup white sugar

1 teaspoon firmly packed light brown sugar

Pre heat oven to 400°F.

Grease a 10 inch fluted flan pan with butter. Roll out the pastry on a lightly-floured counter into a circle 2 inches larger than the flan pan. Ease the pastry into the pan without stretching and press down lightly into the corners and trim the edge. Prick the base with a fork and chill, uncovered, in the refrigerator for 20 to 30 minutes. Line the pastry shell with parchment paper and fill with dried beans. Bake on a pre-heated baking sheet for 15 minutes. Remove the beans and paper and return to the oven for 10 minutes, or until the pastry is dry and just colored. Remove from the oven and reduce the temperature to 300°F.

Put the cornstarch, granulated white sugar, and lemon rind in a pan. Pour in a little of the water and blend to a smooth paste. Gradually add the remaining water and the lemon juice. Bring the mixture to a boil over medium heat, stirring constantly. Simmer gently for 1 minute, or until smooth and glossy. Remove from the heat and beat in the egg yolks, one at a time, then beat in the butter. Put the pan in a bowl of cold water to cool the filling. When cool, spoon into the pastry shell.

For the meringue, whisk the egg whites with an electric mixer until soft peaks form. Add the white sugar gradually, whisking well with each addition, until glossy and firm. Spoon over the filling to cover it completely. Swirl the meringue into peaks and sprinkle with the brown sugar. Bake for 20 to 30 minutes, or until the meringue is crispy and pale gold but still soft in the center.

Something Sweet ✦ 207

Chocolate & Walnut Sponge Cake

serves 4-6

½ cup unsweetened cocoa, plus extra for dusting

2 tablespoons milk

1 cup self-rising flour

pinch of salt

½ cup (1 stick) softened unsalted butter, plus extra for greasing

½ cup sugar

2 eggs, lightly beaten

½ cup chopped walnuts

Whipped cream, to serve

Grease a 5-cup heatproof bowl. Cut out a double circle of wax paper that is 3 inches wider than the rim of the bowl. Grease 1 side with butter and make a pleat in the center.

Mix the cocoa with the milk to a paste in a small bowl. Sift the flour and salt into a separate small bowl.

Beat together the butter and sugar in a large bowl until pale and fluffy. Gradually beat in the eggs, a little at a time, then gently fold in the sifted flour, followed by the cocoa mixture and the walnuts.

Spoon the mixture into the prepared bowl. Cover the bowl with the wax paper circle, buttered-side down, and tie in place with kitchen string. Stand the bowl on a trivet in the slow cooker and pour in enough boiling water to come about halfway up the side of the bowl. Cover and cook on high for 3–3½ hours.

Carefully remove the bowl from the slow cooker and discard the wax paper. Run a knife around the inside of the bowl, then turn out onto a warmed serving dish. Serve immediately with whipped cream, dusted with cocoa.

Crêpes with Apples

serves 4

1 cup all-purpose flour
Pinch of salt
1 teaspoon finely grated lemon zest
1 egg
1¼ cups whole milk
1–2 tablespoons vegetable oil, plus extra, for greasing
Lemon zest, for decorating

Filling

1 cup baking apples, peeled, cored, and sliced
2 tablespoons raisins

Sauce

¼ cup (½ stick) butter
3 tablespoons light corn syrup
⅓ cup firmly packed dark brown sugar
1 tablespoon rum or brandy (optional)
1 tablespoon lemon juice

Preheat the oven to 325°F.

Brush a casserole dish with a little oil.

Sift the flour and salt into a bowl. Add the lemon zest, egg, and milk and whisk to make a smooth batter.

Heat a little oil in a heavy skillet. Make 8 thin crêpes, using extra oil as required. Stack the cooked crêpes, layering them with paper towels or parchment paper, and keep warm.

To make the filling, cook the apples with the raisins in a little water over low heat until soft. Divide the mixture evenly among the crêpes and roll up or fold into triangles. Arrange the crêpes in the casserole dish. Bake for about 15 minutes until warmed through.

To make the sauce, melt the butter, syrup, and sugar together in a pan, stirring well. Add the rum or brandy, if using, and the lemon juice. Do not let the mixture boil.

Serve the crêpes on warmed plates, with a little sauce poured over, and decorated with the lemon zest.

Butterscotch Blondies

makes 9

½ cup (1 stick) butter, melted

¾ cup packed brown sugar

¼ cup white sugar

1 large egg plus 1 egg yolk, beaten together

1 teaspoon vanilla extract

½ teaspoon baking powder

Pinch baking soda

¼ teaspoon salt

1 cup all-purpose flour

½ cup butterscotch chips

¼ cup milk chocolate chips

¼ cup chopped dry-roasted cashews

Pre-heat oven to 350°F.

Add the flour, baking soda, baking powder, and salt to a mixing bowl. Stir with a whisk to combine. Reserve.

In another large mixing bowl, whisk together the melted butter and sugars until combined. Add the eggs and vanilla, and stir to combine. Switch to a wooden spoon and stir in the flour mixture. Fold in the butterscotch chips, chocolate chips, and cashews.

With a spatula, scrape the batter into a lightly greased 8 x 8 inch pan or glass baking dish. Smooth to distribute evenly. Bake for about 35 minutes, or until the top is golden brown and a toothpick inserted in the center comes out clean.

Cool before cutting into 9 bars.

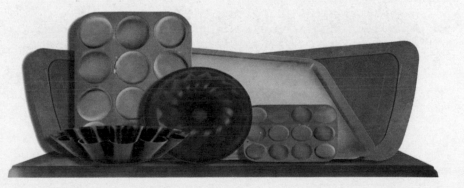

Blushing Pears

6 small ripe pears

1 cup ruby port

1 cup sugar

1 teaspoon finely chopped candied ginger

2 tablespoons lemon juice

Whipped cream or strained plain yogurt, to serve

Peel the pears, cut them in half lengthwise, and scoop out the cores. Place them in the slow cooker.

Combine the port, sugar, ginger, and lemon juice in a pitcher and pour the mixture over the pears. Cover and cook on low for 4 hours, until the pears are tender.

Let the pears cool in the slow cooker, then carefully transfer to a bowl and chill in the refrigerator until required.

To serve, cut each pear half into about 6 slices lengthwise, leaving the fruit intact at the stalk end. Carefully lift the pear halves onto serving plates and press gently to fan out the slices. Spoon the cooking juices over the pears and serve immediately with cream or yogurt.

The most important kitchen utensil is the corkscrew!

Rice Pudding

serves 4

⅔ cup short-grain rice

4 cups whole milk

1½ cups sugar

1 teaspoon vanilla extract

Ground cinnamon, to decorate

Rinse the rice well under cold running water and drain thoroughly. Pour the milk in a large heavy pan, add the sugar, and bring to a boil, stirring constantly. Sprinkle in the rice, stir well, and simmer gently for 10–15 minutes. Transfer the mixture to a heatproof bowl and cover with aluminum foil.

Stand the bowl on a trivet in the slow cooker and pour in enough boiling water to come about one-third of the way up the side of the bowl. Cover and cook on high for 2 hours.

Carefully remove the bowl from the slow cooker and discard the foil. Stir the vanilla extract into the rice, then spoon it into warmed bowls. Lightly dust with cinnamon and serve immediately.

Index